MW00534821

OUT HERE ON OUR OWN

An Oral History of an American Boomtown

J.J. ANSELMI · Photographs by Jordan Utley

University of Nebraska Press

LINCOLN

Chapter 9 first appeared as "The Rise and Fall of a Fracking Boomtown," *New Republic* (December 21, 2020), and is reprinted with permission of the *New Republic*. Portions of Marilyn Nesbit Wood's *The Day the Whistle Blew* (Glendo WY: High Plains Press, 2014) appear courtesy of Debbie Maljian. Portions of Thomas Cullen's *Rock Springs: Growing Up in a Wyoming Coal Town 1915–1938* (Rock Springs WY: Sweetwater County Museum Foundation, 2005) appear courtesy of Sweetwater County Museum Foundation. A portion of "Miners Still Digging in Stansbury Mine in Effort to Find Body" appears with permission of *Rocket Miner*, rocketminer.com.

The University of Nebraska Press is part of a land-grant institution with campuses and programs on the past, present, and future homelands of the Pawnee, Ponca, Otoe-Missouria, Omaha, Dakota, Lakota, Kaw, Cheyenne, and Arapaho Peoples, as well as those of the relocated Ho-Chunk, Sac and Fox, and Iowa Peoples.

Library of Congress Cataloging-in-Publication Data
Names: Anselmi, J. J., author. | Utley, Jordan, photographer.
Title: Out here on our own: an oral history of an American boomtown / J.J. Anselmi; photographs by Jordan Utley.
Description: Lincoln: University of Nebraska Press, [2022] | Includes bibliographical references.
Identifiers: LCCN 2022010521
ISBN 9781496232328 (paperback)
ISBN 9781496234131 (epub)
ISBN 9781496234148 (pdf)
Subjects: LCSH: Rock Springs (Wyo.)—History—Anecdotes. | Rock Springs (Wyo.)—Social conditions. | Oil industry workers—Wyoming—Rock Spring—Interviews. | Coal miners—Wyoming—Rock Spring—Interviews. | BISAC: HISTORY / United States / State & Local / West (AK, CA, CO, HI, ID, MT, NV, UT, WY) | SOCIAL SCIENCE / Race & Ethnic Relations
Classification: LCC F769.R6 A67 2022 | DDC 978.7/85—dc23/eng/20220328
LC record available at https://lccn.loc.gov/2022010521

Set in Minion Pro by Mikala R. Kolander.

For the ones who left early

Contents

Preface

When people ask me about Rock Springs, Wyoming, the wind-worn mining town where I grew up, I tell them about the psychic toll of the boom-bust cycle, the ubiquitous addiction, how terrifyingly common suicide is there, and the extreme drought of mental health resources in the area. When people ask me about Rock Springs, I tell them about the rough-hewn beauty of the high desert and what that land can teach us about survival—and I talk about the sandstone cliffs that, when hit by the sun during the summer months, glow in sherbet fluorescence. I tell stories about my dad, who spent twenty-five years of his life working for Pacific Power and Light—first at the coal-fueled power plant, then as a meter reader, and finally back at the plant, dumping massive trucks of coal ash—until he had to quit because of the damage that work delivered on his body. I mention my grandpa, Don Anselmi, a Rock Springs businessman who, in 1977, was accused by Dan Rather on national television of having connections to organized crime. I talk about all these things and much more, and yet . . . On my own, I feel like I can never paint a full portrait of the inimitable boomtown that has played such a large role in shaping who I am and how I see the world.

To understand Rock Springs, you need to hear a collection of stories told by people who, at one time or another, have called that place home—the stories of raucous partying and violence during the booms, and the stories of crushing hardship and despair during the busts. You need to hear about the wind and forty-below winters, and how you can almost forget that biting cold during the summer. You need to hear about coal mining and backbreaking manual labor in the oil fields. You need to hear people's wrenching stories of addiction and how routine suicide has become for us, which makes it no less devastating. And you need to know how isolating a town like that can be. But you also need to hear the stories of people loving life and doing whatever the fuck they want on the vast stretches of public land that surround Rock Springs—and you need to hear people talk about giving each other everything they can, because that's how you survive in the high desert.

Everyone from Rock Springs knows what a unique town and area it is, but that knowledge can't be embodied in one person's narrative or experience. It's the patchwork of our stories that will show you exactly what we mean when we say Rock Springs is both entirely unique and entirely American.

DAN SHINEBERG: When many people think of Wyoming, they think of Yellowstone, Jackson Hole, and the Grand Tetons. That's just one small section of the state. Rock Springs is a windy desert town on I-80. It's oil workers. Gas workers. Coal miners. And you have a lot of drugs. You don't have the pine trees and picturesque mountains. It's not a place for retirement.

WALT: Honestly, I'm kind of a dysfunctional, barely employable, fucked up mess, and I think that town has a lot to do with it. I moved away in 2013. I tried to forget a lot of what I saw in Rock Springs. Like when I was on my way to work on Pilot Butte and stopped to watch the cops hanging out around a pawn shop. We heard a bang, then they frantically kicked in a window and dove in. Turns out a teenage girl had killed herself. I saw a lot of that: freeway head-on collisions where I was watching the car when it happened; or when a guy running from the cops swerved in my lane and missed hitting me by inches; or in Green River, when police chased a guy on a motorcycle and we followed and saw them removing the body after he hit a pole. I guess I do remember some stuff. That's kind of why I left. I ended up knowing or seeing a lot of shit. Hell, the last weekend before I left, I went to the funeral of a friend and old coworker who shot himself. I only found out when one of the Burns Towing guys mentioned it.

I think the head-on I mentioned was a suicide. It was never in the paper that I know of. The weird part was that I had just broken up with my girlfriend who worked at Walmart, so I was about to leave Walmart. I opened the door to my car, and instead of getting in, I stood there and zoned out. I was staring off and found myself watching a little red car, like Miata little. I had no thoughts whatsoever, just blank. And I didn't realize the car I was watching was in the oncoming lane doing freeway speed until it exploded parts all over the freeway after it slammed head-on into one semi, and then the several semis it was driving next to. It was definitely fatal. The ambulance showed up and the paramedics ran to the car and paused before slowly walking away. It was fucking nuts, and I don't know why I stopped to watch before there was anything to watch. Never heard another thing about it, like it never happened.

NATE MARTIN: The first thing I tell people about Rock Springs is that it's a boomtown. That captures a lot of its overarching realities and helps people understand the character as far as it being a place where people come and go. There's a transient aspect to Rock Springs. No one is working in the tech industry, you know?

It's also a very isolated place. It's in the middle of the Red Desert, and, aside from Green River, it's one hundred miles both ways to the nearest town. That's because of the railroad and the way they would lay one hundred miles of track, make a camp, then lay another hundred miles before the next camp. There was never any reason between the late 1800s and the present day to make any other towns between those one-hundred-mile sections of track.

OUT HERE ON OUR OWN

1

Stolen Land, upon Beds of Coal

As with virtually every other town in the West, Rock Springs began with the original sin of colonization. We killed Indigenous people and stole their land because we found something we wanted: coal. We committed genocide for a form of energy that, in the grand scheme of human history, was only briefly useful but turned out to be endlessly damaging. This is not the way I was taught about my town's history during my childhood; but I wish it had been.

An 1850 survey party led by Howard Stansbury, whose journal entries are excerpted here, discovered coal in the Rock Springs area, a discovery that motivated Union Pacific to lay train tracks there. According to most of my teachers, Stansbury and the white settlers who came after him were brave, resourceful, and strong—which is partly true. But it's also true that they profited from murder and theft.

Playing out in the desert as kids, we'd spot petroglyphs etched in the sandstone cliffs that had somehow resisted erosion.

DUDLEY GARDNER, ARCHEOLOGIST: They've found archaic pit houses in the Rock Springs area from different hunter-gatherer groups. Several Native American groups used to pass through, and the group that was here right before coal was discovered was Shoshone.

There were a lot of animals that passed through, so it was great hunting. There was a lot of buffalo—more than what you might think—as well as antelope, deer, and elk. It was abundant in wildlife.

The trade networks were also well established. All told, there was a sophisticated culture of hunter-gatherers here.

Out north of town, we found a site where a man had been killed. You do have records of people getting shot at and killed. It was land disputes, people fighting for their territory.

There are petroglyphs up on White Mountain and out in the hills. You have them in several of the gaps and canyons as well. There's extensive rock art in the area, and in the Red Desert. People have inhabited this area for over twelve thousand years.

HOWARD STANSBURY, LEADER OF AN 1850 U.S. ARMY SURVEY PARTY: Jim Bridger offered his services as guide, he being well acquainted with the ground over which it was my desire to pass. Our route lay directly through on the ground of powerful tribes ...

We saddled up and started on our journey, directing our course up the valley of Bitter Creek, which enters Green River about a mile below. Crossing the bottom of Bitter Creek Valley, we passed the mouth of Bitter Creek and ascended it the whole day's march. For the first half-dozen miles, the valley is much cut up by deep gullies, worn by the water from the rapidly decomposing hills on each side of the stream . . . So rapid is the disintegration of the sandstone bluffs, and so constant the wash of the soil, that the valley so far is almost entirely destitute of even a spear of grass and presents a most desolate appearance . . .

At a point thirteen miles from the mouth of Bitter Creek, we found a bed of bituminous coal cropping out of the north bluff of the valley, with every indication of it being quite abundant.[1]

THOMAS CULLEN: The decision to locate the railroad in the southern part of Wyoming rather than through South Pass was based, to a great extent, on the existence of coal deposits, which Stansbury had documented ...

The building of the railroad took on the aspect of a military operation. The advance guards were the crews of surveyors and locators. The second line did the grading, bridge building, and cutting through the mountainous country. The main body of men placed the ties, laid the track, spiked the rails down, and added ballast to complete the road. They drank raw whiskey when available and bathed when a stream was handy. The workers were often used to kill [Indigenous people] . . .

The Rock Springs Stage Station was built in 1862 with a Frenchman as its first stationmaster. The station was, no doubt, made of native stone because of the abundance of this building material in the vicinity and the shortage of other suitable building material. The building stood a short distance west of Killpecker Creek near a spring issuing from below a rocky cliff. The original stationmaster was killed by [Native Americans] who mistook him for a soldier. The Blair brothers, Archibald and Duncan, were in charge of the station from 1866 until the Union Pacific Railroad was built through the area . . .

In 1868, to take advantage of the opportunity to supply coal to the railroad, Archibald and Duncan Blair left the stage station and opened a mine at an outcrop on the south side of Bitter Creek. By 1869, men were employed at the new mine, and miner's tents sprang up among the hills. Dugouts were also burrowed into the creek banks near the mine. Miners and their families were housed in tents and dugouts along the banks of Bitter Creek . . .

The general area where the stage station stood was known later as No. 6 and was the site of No. 6 mine, operated by the Union Pacific Coal Department. No. 6 mine was the location of the disturbance between white and Chinese miners, which led to the Chinese Riot in 1885.[2]

ROBERT B. RHODE: It was well-known that the Union Pacific was hiring Chinese [laborers] for its section crews, which did routine track maintenance. It has also hired Chinese [people] to work in its mines . . . in the southwestern corner of Wyoming.

About the time the first Chinese miners arrived . . . the mine boss reported a rifle bullet whizzed by his head as he was standing on the platform of the railroad depot. The shot came, he thought, from the direction of the [white] miners' homes.

. . . The Chinese [miners and their families] settled into huts hastily erected north of Bitter Creek on a sagebrush flat near the No. 3 mine and about a quarter mile north of the center of town. This was quickly dubbed "Chinatown," an accretion of shacks the company had put up plus additions fashioned by the occupants from old boards, packing boxes, and flattened tin cans.[3]

2

Our Animosity

I first learned of the Chinese Massacre of 1885, during which white residents and miners murdered twenty-eight Chinese residents and miners, in grade school. Our fourth-grade class was on a field trip to the local history museum. The tour guide showed us a large mural depicting the atrocity. The mural showed a mob attacking Chinatown, a swath of fire and death in their wake. People trying to escape were cut down by frenzied whites shooting on horseback, or from the safety of nearby bluffs. Plumes of smoke reached from burning shacks into the wide-open sky. White townspeople who didn't partake of the violence watched and cheered.

It was a grisly image to imprint upon the minds of fourth graders—but it told the story honestly. My history teachers occasionally mentioned the massacre in the years afterward, although not in any depth, and not in a way that would become seared in my memory. The following letter was written by those who survived the massacre. Had we read this in school, perhaps the event would have seemed more real to us—and maybe it could have been used as a tool to show that physical violence is never far from racist thought and speech.

RESIDENT OF THE ROCK SPRINGS, WYOMING TERRITORY, 1885: We, the undersigned, have been in Rock Springs, Wyoming Territory, for periods ranging from one to fifteen years, for the purpose of working on the railroads and in the coal mines . . . Several times we had been approached by the white men and requested to join them in asking the companies for an increase in the wages of all, both Chinese and white men. We inquired of them what we should do if the companies refused to grant an increase. They answered that if the companies would not increase our wages we should all strike . . . To this we dissented, wherefore we excited their animosity against us . . .

About two o'clock in the afternoon a mob, divided into two gangs, came toward "Chinatown," one gang coming by way of the plank bridge, and the other by way of the railroad bridge . . . One squad remained at Coal Shed No. 3 and another at the pump house. The squad that remained at the pump house fired the first shot, and the squad that stood at Coal Shed No. 3 immediately followed their example and fired. The Chinese man by the name of Lor Sun Kit was the first person shot, and fell to the ground. At that time the Chinese began to realize that the mob were bent on killing . . . Soon after, the mob on the hill behind Coal Pit No. 3 came down from the hill, and joining the different squads of the mob, fired their weapons and pressed on to Chinatown . . .

Whenever the mob met a Chinese man they stopped him and, pointing a weapon at him, asked him if he had any revolver, and then approaching him they searched his person, robbing him of his watch or any gold or silver that he might have about him, before letting him go. Some of the rioters would let a Chinese man go after depriving him of all his gold and silver, while another would be beaten with the butt ends of the weapons before being let go. Some of the rioters, when they could not stop a Chinese man, would shoot him dead on the spot and then search and rob him. Some would overtake a Chinese man, throw him down, and search and rob him before they would let him go. Some of the rioters would not fire their weapons but would only use the butt ends to beat the Chinese with. Some would not beat a man but rob him of whatever he had and let him go, yelling to him to go quickly. Some, who took no part either in beating or robbing the Chinese, stood by, shouting loudly and laughing and clapping their hands. There was a gang of women that stood at the "Chinatown" end of the plank bridge and cheered; among the women, two of them each fired successive shots at the Chinese . . .

The Chinese who were the first to flee mostly dispersed themselves at the back hills, on the opposite bank of the creek, and among the opposite hills . . . Every one of them was praying to Heaven or groaning with pain . . .

Between 4:00 p.m. and a little past 9:00 p.m., all the camp houses belonging to the coal company and the Chinese huts had been burned down completely, only one of the company's camp houses remaining . . . After having been killed, the dead bodies of some were carried to the burning buildings and thrown into the flames. Some of the Chinese who had hid themselves in the houses were killed and their bodies burned; some, who on account of sickness could not run, were burned alive in the houses . . .

The whole number of Chinese killed was twenty-eight and those wounded fifteen . . . On behalf of those killed or wounded, or of those deprived of their property, we pray that the examining commission will ask our minister to sympathize, and to endeavor to secure the punishment of the murderers, the relief of the wounded, and compensation for those despoiled of their property, so that the living and the relatives of the dead will be grateful . . .

Hereinabove we have made a brief recital of the facts of this riot, and pray your honor will take them into your kind consideration. Here follow the signatures of 559 Chinese laborers, residents at Rock Springs, Wyoming Territory.[1]

3

With Blackened Lungs

In his memoir, *Rock Springs: Growing Up in a Wyoming Coal Town 1915–1938*, Thomas Cullen describes his father's experience working in Rock Springs coal mines at the turn of the twentieth century— and, for him personally, what it was like to not know whether his dad would make it home each day. Compared to the death traps miners toiled in back then, today's coal mines are much safer, although still hazardous.

There's a tendency among educated, white-collar workers like me (particularly men) to romanticize the type of life-threatening labor Cullen describes. But Cullen's father didn't want his son to have anything to do with coal mining. For Pa Cullen, there was no romance in his occupation, just the promise of black lung and bodily harm. The salt in those wounds was that the higher-ups of the mining companies would never themselves be exposed to such dangers.

As Cullen and others describe here, many miners and residents soothed their pain with alcohol. Then, as now, suicide was a fact of life for people who lived in Rock Springs.

THOMAS CULLEN: Pa left Butte, going south to Rock Springs, where he found employment as a miner at the Union Pacific Coal Company's No. 10 mine. Rock Springs was tough, dirty, and mean, but we loved it—warts and all. I grew up with the feeling that it was somehow disloyal to harbor thoughts of leaving Rock Springs . . .

In the beginning, mining methods were crude. The coal was

undercut with hand picks and shot with black powder. Pit cars were hauled by mules to outside, where the coal was loaded into wagons and hauled to the railroad. Both horses and mules were used to gather pit cars . . . Coal from Blairtown Mine was hauled up the steep main slope to the tipple by means of hoist and cable. When the loaded trips reached the tipple, the pit cars were dumped and the rope rider rode back down the slope, hunched down between the pit cars of the empty trip . . .

Since there was little ventilation in the mines, the air became thick with acrid smoke . . . Many deaths from accidents occurred in the mines, but it was reported that most deaths resulted from fights. Charles Wardell, who helped found Rock Springs . . . became involved in an argument and was slashed across the abdomen by Bobby Frew. Wardell obtained a gun and fatally shot Frew . . .

Occasionally, when walking around on Sunday afternoons, we were alerted by sounds of a brass band coming up the street and we immediately ran to the source of the music to learn that the band was often playing for a miner's funeral.

In a word, the old company house was cold in winter. Pa cut down on the heat loss from drafty floors by shoveling dirt around the lower part of the outside walls to prevent the wind from getting under the house . . .

Nora was born March 15, 1917, and died in January 1920 from convulsions due to teething. Pa built a shadowbox measuring three feet square by eight inches, closed on one side, with a glass door on the front side . . . In April 1921, my sister Mary died from uremic poisoning—a complication of tonsillitis . . . One of Mom's doctors told her that kids living in Rock Springs were exposed to more diseases than their counterparts living in a milder, more favorable climate . . .

One day, Kathleen had her face frozen while returning to school. When she had no feeling in her cheeks, she scratched deeply with her fingernail, resulting in small scars to remind her of the storm.

The cuts on miners' hands and fingers healed over the coal dust, leaving blue markings curiously similar to an ordinary tattoo. I'm satisfied that the blue markings on the backs of Pa's hands and fingers were, in fact, miner's tattoos . . .

Many times, when Pa took me to the mine in the evening after supper, we often stayed until quite late . . . A white horse stood by to haul the loaded pit cars to the main haulage-way to be hauled by hoist and cable to the surface. Pa repeatedly warned me about touching the electric wires attached to the roof or to timbers lining the tunnels . . .

Nearly everything associated with Pa's clothes or mining equipment was given the name "pit." He referred to his clothes worn to the mine as pit clothes. His heavy woolen socks were pit socks. His shirt was his pit shirt . . .

I knew the long work hours were wearing on Pa. Many times, I heard him softly say, "Gosh, I'm tired," as he leaned forward in his kitchen chair, rubbing his hands through his hair before going downstairs to shower before supper . . .

I don't think Prohibition was taken seriously in Rock Springs.[1]

LES GEORGIS: During Prohibition, my grandparents dug a still into the dirt of a hill. My grandmother made whiskey out of grape mash, and my grandpa used to put saddlebags on a horse and get his wagon and ride to meet guys from Colorado and sell alcohol to them.

ROBERT B. RHODE: In the Rock Springs-Green River area during the Prohibition Era, more than one hundred raids were made on private homes, soft drink parlors (the Rock Springs version of the speakeasy), and stills hidden in buildings or caves.[2]

THOMAS CULLEN: After [one] still was located and the arrest made, the bootlegger, Mike Soptick, requested permission to return to his cabin to get his coat. Permission was granted. Soptick came out of the cabin with a rifle. Agent Capen was shot and mortally wounded. Epperson shot Soptick, killing him instantly. Jim Capen died before reaching the hospital . . .

Beginning in September, carloads of California wine grapes were sold from $70 to $110 a ton from refrigerated cars, spotted on the siding, to members of the Italian community, who hauled them by truck to their homes.

LES GEORGIS: My wife's grandpa who worked in the mines, he killed himself. He shot himself in the basement. He was of the old Italian persuasion, [the type of person] who made wine and drank it. I remember my dad and uncles saying my grandfather couldn't keep food in the house, but he could go to the railroad tracks to get his grapes. My wife's grandfather was convinced that he was going to die of cancer, he drank a lot, and he was tired of living. He was retired from the mines, and he'd gotten some black lung.

MARGARET NESBIT: For a while there, I thought I just couldn't do this. I [didn't] want to face any of this. I was looking for something in the medicine cabinet to drink to make all this stop. I wanted to die.[3]

THOMAS CULLEN: An older transient, often noticed in the downtown area, slept under the bandstand near the Rialto Theater. He often went to the kitchen door at Our Lady of Sorrows rectory where he was given a sandwich. Later, he was found dead, hanging from a rope at Gilpin field. The story was that he had been robbed of his small savings and was despondent . . .

[Another] suicide occurred just off the depot platform on the Union Pacific mainline. It seems the station agent observed a few transients sleeping on benches in the waiting room, woke them, and turned them out into the cold. One disgruntled young transient left the depot in what must have been an agitated state, throwing himself under the wheels of a passing train. Harry Henkel and I arrived just as the ambulance was leaving with the mangled body. As we passed the depot, we saw one of the victim's shoes still lying, cut in two, between the rails.

RAY SILVESTRI: It's tough to know exactly why the suicide rate there is high. The ones I've known were these older coal miners that had become ill, and they didn't want to deal with trying to hang on forever. They decided it was time. That was the case with my dad.

THOMAS CULLEN: Pa knew from long experiences in the mines in England and in Illinois, Kansas, and Wyoming that the cost of coal was often measured in broken bodies, fatalities, and bereaved families. If a miner survived cave-ins, gas explosions, and fires, he fell heir to miner's asthma, miner's knee, and black lung. Pa suffered a broken hip from a fall of coal early in his mining career. This injury bothered him all his working life . . .

Pa didn't encourage young kids, just out of high school, to go into the coal mines. I know that he went out of his way to discourage them from doing so. Sven Swanson, with whom I played sandlot sports when we were kids, mentioned that he had asked Pa several times about a job in Blairtown Mine but was always told that he would be better off to look elsewhere . . .

Pa's efforts to pit his strength, bone, and muscle against the stubborn and unrelenting Wyoming prairie failed. The old mines have been sealed and flooded.

4
Where We're From

During the first half of the twentieth century, people in Rock Springs did everything they could to make the hardscrabble area their home. Met with unceasing wind, subzero winters, hazardous work conditions, and stingy mining companies, citizens survived through community. From neighbors sharing food to the formation of the miners' union, it was people's ability to band together and help each other that enabled them to thrive in such an inhospitable place. At some point, we collectively bought into the idea that rugged individualism is the key to survival in the West. But that has never been the case.

Even if you had strong community bonds, however, Rock Springs could be brutal. The people interviewed here have deep ties to the town, and their lives have been shaped by those ties.

JACK WATERS: You know as well as I do that it takes a special kind of person to live and grow up here. I live in the house my great-grandpa built in 1913. It looks like the house from *Amityville Horror*—I love it. My great-grandpa was one of the first Union Pacific mining superintendents they brought out here; he had a huge family.

WING LEW: My great-grandfather moved from China to Idaho. He wanted to find better work, so he moved to Rock Springs. He helped my dad come over when he was eleven.

My dad actually had a paper father who lived somewhere else and helped him get here. So he was here illegally, then he studied to get his citizenship and went through that process. He eventually graduated from Rock Springs High School, back when it was in the building downtown, and went on to own a successful restaurant. My mother moved here from Hong Kong and really didn't like it. She'd moved to this tiny prairie town after living in one of the world's biggest cities.

JOAN: It was bleak and desolate. There wasn't much greenery around here. For the most part, Bunning's Park was the only green area. There was no grass in my grandma's yard. Maybe it was the cost of water, but there wasn't much greenery on the streets, either.

LES GEORGIS: My dad was born in No. 2 camp in 1917. They've torn down most of those old mining camps now. My grandpa used to live in the camp, and he worked in the mines along with two of his brothers. He immigrated from Italy sometime in the late 1890s. The town was all immigrants. Both my wife's grandparents and mine immigrated from Italy. My wife's grandpa also worked in the mines.

When we were kids, we'd find pieces of Chinese pottery down in the creek.

JESSE REED: Part of my family came here because of coal. My mother, Pearl, was from Illinois, and she was married to Jesse Reed, who came here to work on the railroad, which he did for a lot of years. I was adopted when I was two weeks old. I never met my real mom.

Oh yeah, I've experienced racism in Rock Springs. It's here, same as anywhere else. Most of the Black families in town have lived here for years, so everybody knew us. Word would get out about racist people. Everybody knew who they were. A lot of the Black people here are related, somehow or someway. That's the story of everyone in Rock Springs, I guess.

DAN SHINEBERG: My dad's family came from Ukraine and Lithu-ania. They moved to the United States in the early 1900s and settled at first in Los Angeles. My great-grandparents on my mom's side were from Germany, and, with stolen passports and documents, were able to flee [from the Nazis]. They moved to New York and then Los Angeles, where they started a cleaners [business]. Then they moved to Rock Springs because they'd already been there and thought they could make money servicing the area with the Union Pacific coal mines. That's when they opened Shineberg's Cleaners.

RAY SILVESTRI: Both of my parents were immigrants. My dad came from Tuscany, and my mom from Northern Italy. They both ended up in Rock Springs, though from different paths. My mom's father was the first in our family to go to Rock Springs. He worked in the mines, then he sent for his family back in Italy.

My dad started out working on the railroad outside Rock Springs, in Point of Rocks. He'd worked in a few other states as well. He ended up getting a permanent job in the mines in Rock Springs, which is where he spent his life.

Before meeting my dad, my mother had married a man in Salt Lake and had my half-brother. Her first husband was killed in a mine explosion in 1923. My brother was only an infant at that time. My grandparents were living in Rock Springs, so she came back to live with them. That's when my dad and mom got together. They had another son who died from influenza. Then I came along in 1934.

Since my dad was a coal miner, we lived in a company house down in what they called No. 4, on Ninth Street. Living there was pretty basic. They were small houses with no indoor plumbing. Everyone made the best of it, though. Our neighbors and everyone around us were all hardworking people. During World War II, everyone had a big garden and grew pretty much everything they needed as far as fruit and vegetables.

The No. 4 area was tough. It was all coal miners, so the kids were tough, too.

LES GEORGIS: I remember going to visit my uncle in the company house. The UP Coal houses were stark. They were clapboard, and I remember the linoleum being all worn out. The lighting was simply a bare bulb hanging from the ceiling. To turn it on, you had to reach up and turn the switch on the light bulb. My uncle lived there until sometime in the fifties. Along with him, three or four families still lived there. There were still houses, but most of them were vacant and falling down, with weeds taking over the yards.

I used to listen to KVRS with my uncle. They had the mine schedules, which opened with a very characteristic *bong, bong, bong.* If you were at anybody's house whose dad worked in the mines, you knew to shut up when they read the schedules. They listened closely to see if they'd be working the next day. The radio people said things like, "No. 12 will be idle tomorrow. No. 13 will be idle. No. 2 will work first and second shift." I can still hear that voice.

When I was a kid, we moved to a house on Pine Street. Everybody around there had coal chutes and burned coal in their houses.

MARILYN NESBIT WOOD: The miners' wives had the responsibility of running their households: tending children, cooking, baking their own bread and pastries, and cleaning. In addition, they tackled the family laundry using primitive conventional washing machines and water heated on the kitchen coal stove. The wives were plumbers, carpenters, peacemakers, teachers, beauticians, and sometimes even dentists and physicians.[1]

MARCIA HENSLEY: The type of work women did in those camps changed traditional roles, certainly for those coming from Europe. You had the New Woman idea gaining traction, which was a more liberated view of the types of work women could do.

DEE GARCEAU: First-generation immigrant women kept house for miners without families, an economic role that doubled as the locus of social networks crucial to immigrant survival. Among the second generation, some women left housekeeping for retail and office work, positions that symbolized Americanization and New Womanhood . . .

Finally, during the second two decades of the twentieth century, single rural women found in homesteading both economic opportunity and a symbolic redefinition of gender. Some wrote about homesteading as a transformation of female identity, drawing on popular mythology about the West as a place of self-reinvention.[2]

ELINORE PRUITT STEWART: There is a saddle horse especially for me and a little shotgun with which I am to kill sage chickens. We are between two trout streams, so you can think of me as being happy when the snow is through melting and the water gets clear.[3]

JOAN: We had an LDS mayor at one point, and girls weren't allowed to go into town in shorts. We had to be properly dressed to go anywhere.

MARILYN NESBIT WOOD: The women came from varied ethnic backgrounds, thus sometimes creating a language barrier. But the sameness of their lives, the sharing of isolation, and the underlying danger of a miner's work unified them.[4]

JAY ANSELMI: My grandpa, Nono, came over from Italy in 1923. He died before you were born. His brother, Olivo, came to Rock Springs in 1921, and he told Nono about all the work in the coal mines. Word got out across the world about working in the mines in Rock Springs. Nono worked in the coal mines for eighteen years. He had polio when he was young, so he walked with a bit of a limp. He was a very strong guy and hard worker. He opened two saloons and quit his coal mining job when the saloons started doing well.

Grandma Lillie was a schoolteacher from Hanna, Wyoming. Her dad died in the Hanna mining explosion. Something like a hundred miners died in that one.

MARILYN NESBIT WOOD: When we got to the portal, everyone stopped and stood in silence on the hill above the mine waiting to hear what had happened and who was hurt. The silence was deafening as the mantrip came out of the mine. I thought how horrific it would be to get news that my father had been injured in a mine accident, or worse yet, had been killed.[5]

THOMAS CULLEN: An explosion at the Frontier coal mine on August 14, 1923, cost the lives of ninety-nine miners. Pa was seated at the kitchen table reading aloud to Mom. From time to time, his voice faltered with emotion, choking up as he read accounts of brothers volunteering to go into the gas-filled mine to attempt the rescue of their brothers.[6]

LES GEORGIS: The way the mines and mining companies treated people was really something. My wife's grandma worked in a boarding house in Salt Lake City, and that's where she met her first husband. He got a job in the coal mines. A lot of people came because they had a connection to someone here, and, many times, that's how they'd get their jobs.

There was an explosion in the Frontier mine near Kemmerer that killed a lot of miners. My wife's grandfather was killed in that explosion. They filled an entire hall with the bodies and had a mass funeral. The miners were laid out like cordwood.

My wife's grandma had been living in a coal camp house, and she had a little baby. The coal company told her that, since her husband wasn't around to work in the mine anymore, she had to move out. They put all her stuff out on the street. I knew another family that happened to as well.

MARILYN NESBIT WOOD: The local bars were filled with distraught miners vocalizing their disgust with the company they had worked for so hard—for so long—and how it was treating them.[7]

JOE BOZNER: Every damn move you make is dangerous. But you just go to work each day hoping to hell today isn't the day the good Lord means for you to get yours.[8]

JOAN: My grandfather moved to America from England when he was five. His family went to Pennsylvania first, then to Colorado. At some point, he made his way to Rock Springs to work in the coal mines. He actually lost his arm in the mine, but that was before I was born. He was handling six, or maybe seven, children. There was no money when he lost his arm—the company didn't provide anything. He lost his arm between the shoulder and elbow, and he walked out of the mine.

Later on, he went to work for the school district. He was a janitor at the high school for many years. I don't remember him talking about the accident. At that time, it was generally understood that you don't air your troubles for everyone to hear. People from that time didn't do that unless you asked them the question. We were just kids and accepted what it was without questioning it. My cousin, whose mother died when she was five, lived with our grandparents, and they raised her. She knew a lot more about what happened there, but unfortunately she's not with us anymore. There was no money or support from the company, and they weren't living in company housing. This was before John Lewis came in and got started with the unions. The idea of the company taking care of people was not something you thought about.

My grandmother was a midwife and later on worked at the hospital as an aide. My grandfather did well with one arm—until he was killed in 1948 on a road going north. He was taking my mother to Jackson because she'd gotten a job in one of the fancy restaurants there. On their way back, he lost control of the car—and of course had only one arm. He rolled it and was killed, but my grandmother survived.

LES GEORGIS: There used to be a lot of reverence for John L. Lewis, who organized the miners' union in Rock Springs. One highlight of my wife's great-grandpa's life was that he went to Squaw Creek, which is where the miners all used to vacation—they used to fondly call it Wop Creek because that's where all the Italians went—with John Lewis. He talked about it for years. When I was a kid, I'd see a picture of this random guy in all the miners' houses. Then I finally realized it was John Lewis.

RAY SILVESTRI: We did well in the No. 4 camp for a time. My dad added a room onto the company house. Like everyone else, he also dug a cantina, which was a wine cellar. Everybody made wine. Our whole neighborhood was first-generation European. There was so much demand for wine that they brought it in on rail cars. People would chip in to buy a ton of grapes, then they'd have a neighborhood get-together to make the wine because only a few people owned a crusher or a press. They would share with each other and help each other load and unload. That was part of life.

There were a lot of bars. My dad had wine on the table every day. It was the lifestyle.

JAY ANSELMI: Nono would buy grapes from California and smash them in his basement to make wine. They'd wear boots, smash them with their feet. They made red and white wine, beer, and whiskey. That cellar where they did it is still there, a hundred years later.

Nona used to cuss in Italian when she'd get mad. The adults spoke Italian when they didn't want kids to understand. My other grandma spoke Finnish when she didn't want us to know what she was talking about.

JOAN: Some of these places didn't want the wives in there. That's where my husband did a lot of his drinking, in those types of bars.

There's always been a lot of alcoholism in Rock Springs, and that's trickled down to my son, who's now twenty-seven years sober with AA. Alcohol was so easily available. It was on every corner. And with a lot of those bars, you didn't go to buy a drink—you went to buy a drunk.

MARILYN NESBIT WOOD: Men outnumbered women in Rock Springs and houses of prostitution thrived. Ladies of the evening, or "K Street ladies," as they were called, lived in apartments in old buildings, often above local businesses. A red light earmarked a street-level entry door with a flight of steps leading upstairs. The establishments were listed in the telephone directory under "Furnished Rooms for Rent," with names such as the Lux Rooms, the Capitol, or the M&M Rooms. On Saturday night, women sat on their windowsills with red velvet drapery blowing in the air around them, or occupied stools in saloons. Many were beautiful women, some very young, and they wore low-cut, fancy dresses, heavy makeup, fishnet hose, spiked heels, and lots of perfume. When they shopped in the local stores, they did not meet the eyes of the wives of the community, who would never have smiled or spoken to them.[9]

RAY SILVESTRI: My folks ended up doing a bit better. They saved up and bought a house up above mine No. 3. I was about eleven when we moved there. That was a big improvement, because now we had indoor plumbing.

My dad worked in the coal mine for as long as I can remember, since before I was born. It was very difficult and dangerous work. My half-brother's dad died in the Frontier mine explosion, and my grandpa was killed in No. 4 by one of the coal cars. My dad had several injuries. He lost a couple fingers and had lifelong back injuries. He worked up until they closed the mine. He worked No. 8 most of his career, and then he worked at the Stansbury mine for a short time. People had been telling him to retire for years.

JOAN: I was living near the Stansbury mine when the cave-in happened and that guy was killed. My husband at the time worked in the mine. He was what they called a rider, and his job was to take the line of cars down into the mine, throw a switch, and then hop back on the cars and take them back up. It was a dangerous job. The lines of cars would move very quickly. You had to be fast to do that and not get hurt. But he really didn't like being in the mines. He didn't stay with that job very long.

LOUIS JULIUS: Johnny told us to move out. "Let's get the hell out of here!" We were going to have three timbers across the face. The roof was good. We had one safety timber up. We were going to put up two more so they could plug it.

There was no warning. The roof behind me fell, an enormous underground thunder, and I started to run. Some rocks were falling in front of me. I ran into something and fell. Johnny was a foot right behind me. I was knocked part way under the loading boom of the Joy Loader. I crawled a little farther in. I asked Johnny how he was. He complained of his back and said, "I'm a goner, Julius."

The second cave-in came. My legs were buried to the knees, I was lying on my stomach. I called to Johnny again. But he didn't answer anymore, just moaned once or twice. I didn't think there would be any more cave-ins after that second time. It had fallen as tight as it was going to. Then all movement and sound ended as abruptly as it had begun. An absolute quiet filled the site which was every bit as loud as the cave-in.

I saw a pant leg and reached down for it. It was mine. I started to dig with my hands to get the circulation going. It was cold, but

I didn't have any trouble breathing. I was conscious all the time. Got dizzy a couple of times, but I'd started moving around, digging with my hands, trying to move my legs. That kept me warm.

I realized I still had my goggles on. I took the damn things off and threw them aside. There was a mine hat lying a little ways from me. I kept looking at it and wondering if it was mine. I asked them when they came to dig me out. They said it was Johnny's.[10]

MARILYN NESBIT WOOD: The next evening, we returned to the mortuary for viewing and saw Daddy for the first time since the accident. For the first hour, only family and relatives were allowed in the sanctuary. We clutched each other when we saw him lying in the casket with coal dust still on his scalp under his wavy black hair, and the crying began all over again. We had to keep touching him, kissing his cheek, laying our hands on his.

Of all the people who came to pay their respects at our home, the mortuary, or the funeral, the superintendent who had sent Daddy to get the last bit of coal out of the ill-fated No. 7 seam was not one of them.

Everyone asked Momma the same questions, and when they didn't, she asked them of herself. "Where are we going to live now that we have to move out of the company house? How can I raise my children and hold us together? How am I going to have enough money?" We all knew families had only a few days to move from the company-owned houses after they were no longer employed by UP Coal.[11]

RAY SILVESTRI: The quality of the doctors in Rock Springs left a lot to be desired. My dad had a bleeding ulcer, and they put him in the hospital, but he wasn't getting any better. My mom decided to take him to Salt Lake, even though the doctor in Rock Springs told her she was wasting her money. They didn't know he had a bleeding ulcer until he got to Salt Lake. They diagnosed him, put him on a diet, and sent him home. He was fine a couple months later. In those days, things like that were scary when they happened.

My dad killed himself, so I think the suicide rate was fairly high then, too. I agonized over that for a long time. He'd been talking about it for years. He served on an Italian community organization that would go around when its members were sick. So he'd seen a lot of people who were ready to die, and he watched them die. He never wanted to be in that bad of a condition. That was his mental approach.

It was sad, because he had some medical problems in his seventies, but he didn't have faith in the doctors. Suicide was his way out. That was his thinking. I forgave him for doing that, even though it was a big shock. But I understand where he was coming from. That approach was part of the old-school mentality. They'd say, "Well, they shoot horses, don't they?"

JOAN: My first husband's great-grandfather hung himself. I'm not sure why, other than his business was competing with another and maybe not doing so well. His daughter, my mother-in-law, was quite a force to be reckoned with. She loaded up a wagon and went south of town to start a ranch, and that's where she raised her sons.

There was a lot of addiction in their family. My first husband eventually became an alcoholic. They found him frozen to death in Bitter Creek when he was thirty-nine. His younger brother shot himself before that. He and his wife had separated, and he was living at his mom's house with his daughter, who was eleven or twelve. He and his daughter got into some kind of argument because he wanted her to do something, and she didn't want to do it. She might've heard the shot, I'm not exactly sure, but she ran to the garage and found her dad.

I know we have a high suicide rate. We've always had the booms and busts. Everybody loses their job about every fifteen years. I lived next door to a family who lost their granddaughter to suicide, but she wasn't living in Rock Springs at the time. I think her father might've killed himself. Addiction can turn into a form of suicide. That's what my husband did: he drank himself to death.

LES GEORGIS: My wife and I had a friend who killed himself just before graduation. He was a really nice guy. His mom was an alcoholic. He would work all night in the Park Hotel. He'd go to school during the day and then work as a bellhop at night. He was making the house payments and earning money for himself, his brother, and sister. I think everything became too much for him. He went out by the old fairgrounds and shot himself.

There were two or three kids who died by suicide right after high school, and then a couple more died in a car wreck. Within a year after we graduated, there were seven or eight kids dead from our senior class. The suicide rate there is a real kicker.

***

JAY ANSELMI: Grandpa John was born and raised in Rock Springs. Him and his brother, Angelo, used to travel to California and bring fruit back to sell. That's how he got his start. He went from there to start his own car dealership. He was a self-made man with a sixth-grade education. He loved to shoot trap and golf, and he was one of the best fly fishermen around. His sons became successful businessmen in Rock Springs, too.

JACK WATERS: We all heard the stories about Grandpa Anselmi bringing in all the Cadillacs with their trunks loaded with booze and selling them to the ranchers and farmers.

LES GEORGIS: In the town, everybody traded with each other. Your great-grandfather, John Anselmi, started Standard Motors there on Elk Street. My two uncles owned a gas station right by there. I remember your great-uncle, Billy, coming over to talk to my uncle, Vinny. Later on, I worked for my father-in-law in his auto parts store. My dad had the little Modern Auto Clinic down there. I remember cars coming in from your great-grandpa's lot.

My dad worked his ass off forever and was pretty successful with his small business. Forty-seven years in it and he got $42,000 out of the business. That's how it was back then.

ALICIA: My family is a middle link between two prominent Black families in Rock Springs. My grandmother ran Sweets' Cafe from 1946 until 1993. They were known for having the best ribs in Wyoming. My grandfather purchased land over time from Judge Hamm. When my grandmother passed away, our family owned eighty-six acres of land around where the cafe was. One of my grandmothers had nine children, and the other had twelve. When I asked my mom why they had so many kids, she said, "What else is there to do here?"

My grandpa came down from Iowa to work in the coal mines. My grandma cooked very well, and they were able to purchase a small plot of land and build the restaurant. When Grandpa got injured, the restaurant became their main source of income.

CHRIS SCHMIDT: My grandpa was a blue-collar laborer. He wanted to get a job in the mines, but he was already pretty old by the time he moved to Rock Springs. He ended up dying in his midfifties, so I never actually met him. He was a hard drinker and smoker, and he died of a heart attack. He moved to Rock Springs to work in one of the mines but was never able to get a solid position. So he bounced around to different jobs.

RAY SILVESTRI: Rock Springs taught me to have a strong work ethic: you work hard, and no matter what the job is, you tackle it. I think my grandkids could benefit from that mentality.

When I was five or six years old, my friend and I ended up at the dummy shack one day. It was a place where they filled these small paper bags with sand. They were used in the mines to back up the dynamite shots. You'd drill a hole, put in the dynamite, and then put in the packet, which they called dummies.

Anyway, my friend and I were playing, and we ended up at the dummy shack. We saw some older boys who were more of a rowdy Rock Springs bunch. They had subcontracted with the old man who normally filled the dummies. So we came along, and those older boys subcontracted to us so we'd do all the work. We were so industrious that we didn't get home for supper. When my dad found us, he was pretty pissed and asked what the hell we were doing down there. We just said, "We're making money!"

After that, my friends and I raised rabbits that we'd use for food and sell to the market. We knew the woman who worked at the bakery and ran the bread slicing machine. I would help her out, and my reward was that I could take the cardboard box from under the slicer where pieces of bread fell. I would drag that box down the street to feed my rabbits.

My brother was an accomplished accordionist. My folks were interested in me learning to play music, so they took me down to get a saxophone when I was in junior high. My friends and I started playing big band music, and we would play a few gigs in dancehalls. We played at Toastmaster's, which is still in business, and we also played at the Park Hotel. We made money, so that was another job I had. The musician's union was still in business at that time; the base pay was ten dollars for a three-hour gig. I also worked at the service station for forty-five cents an hour.

JOAN: We didn't have a lot here. We had no major sports, no swimming pool. We had to create our own entertainment. And when I was a kid, we didn't have a lot of vehicles either. When my cousin and I were eleven or twelve, we decided to go out in the hills one morning and cook our breakfast. We told our parents we were going to do it—and we did it. We brought water in this container we carried between us, and we brought groceries and a cast iron skillet. We had bacon, bread, and eggs. We walked down the highway outside town to a grouping of rocks. Our family only had the one car; you didn't just ask for rides. Anyway, we walked about a mile and cooked our breakfast. What eleven or twelve-year-old today would be allowed to do that? We used to walk all over town, even around nine or ten o'clock at night.

MARILYN NESBIT WOOD: As the snow melted, the whole area became a muddy mess. Many times we got stuck in the clay-like mud and had to be careful not to slide over the edge of the hill while getting up to the house.[12]

JOAN: I've lived and visited other places like Oregon, Washington, and California. I don't care for cities. I've lived in Denver and Salt Lake, and I didn't like it much. I've sometimes wondered if there's an umbilical cord between me and Rock Springs. I keep getting drawn back here.

It's high desert country, and you have to get used to it. You either like it or you don't. Some people think it's still the Wild West and that we all ride horses. In Michigan, these people heard that my sister is from Wyoming and asked her about all the cowboys, so she said, "Yeah, we all ride horses everywhere." She really had them going, but then she got worried someone was going to offer to take her horseback riding.

My friend moved here from Arizona, and when she told her friends there she was leaving, one of them said, "Well, where is Wyoming?" She said it's the state above Colorado. The woman said, "No, it isn't. Montana is the state above Colorado." My friend had a hard time convincing her that Wyoming was even a real place.

LES GEORGIS: Rock Springs is only there because it had water—and it had coal. When they were building the transcontinental railroad, Union Pacific owned every other section of land, so they ended up owning a lot of coal mines. The steam engines burned coal back then. But in the early 1950s, the trains went to diesel/electric, the diesel engines that run electric motors, which is what they still use today. When Union Pacific made that shift, the demand for coal dropped immensely. Both of my uncles lost their jobs. Everybody was sure Rock Springs would become a ghost town. Lots of people moved away.

MARILYN NESBIT WOOD: 1954 was a devastating year for the coal industry in Wyoming. A vast amount of coal lay underground, but there wasn't a big market for it anymore. Rumors began spreading throughout the camps that Union Pacific had 190 diesel engines on order.

I looked across the table at Daddy and wondered what he would do if that diesel engine did put him out of a job. Where would we go?

Things fell like dominoes once the Reliance Mine closed: the Hanna mine closed, the Stansbury school closed, the bus line quit running, the boarding house closed. The miners at Stansbury and Superior, where the mines still operated, could see the end was near. Kids looked forward to summer, but the summer recreation program—including the baseball league—had closed down. The only part left was the Friday swim at the Rock Springs High School swimming pool . . .

I noticed miners listening even more closely to the evening mine schedule report on KVRS radio. Radio announcers Imogene Parr and Michael Read, who were already household names for reporting daily mine schedules, became more important to the hourly miners than ever before.[13]

JOAN: I worked for the school district, in the superintendent's office. We were a poor school district. The eastern side of Wyoming had more money. Then all of a sudden, trona was discovered, and money came into Rock Springs. The eastern Wyoming towns realized they should get into trona, too. The state organized it so there would be an equitable division of resources: the trona money got dispersed throughout the state to any district that needed it.

LES GEORGIS: The trona mines came in to replace some of the coal jobs, but I don't recall there being a boom. Texas Gulf Sulfur came in after a few trona mines opened, then so did Church & Dwight.

A number of my friends and their dads worked in the coal mines. When I was in high school, that's when the coal mines really began to close down. The trona mines and natural gas with Mountain Fuel took up some of the slack; but again, it wasn't really a boom.

When the mines closed and my wife's step-grandpa got laid off, he was close to retirement. His wife went to work cleaning houses and doing laundry at an old age because that's what she had to do. She came here when she was seventeen. She taught herself to read and write English. We have a bunch of her letters, and you can see how she taught herself by spelling phonetically.

It's a tough little town. People have survived and found a way. Part of that is the immigrant mentality. My grandpa lived through the Depression and instilled that mindset into me. If you grew up here, it's hard to fathom how tough you'd have to be to move to a totally different country where you don't know the language, where you don't know the customs, and where you're totally at the mercy of the people who might hire you.

MARILYN NESBIT WOOD: All the while I was growing up, I'd thought there would always be a Stansbury, just like there would always be a Rock Springs. Never in my wildest dreams did I think the day would come when Stansbury would be completely obliterated . . .

As the car turned the final bend to approach the camp, I gasped in disbelief. All that was left was a graveyard of foundations. Like an oasis on a desert, our house stood alone on its foundation. The wind in all its fury swept and howled eerily through the rubble . . .

The following summer, rumors began to spread around Rock Springs that hippie teenagers were living in the vacant foundations in Stansbury.[14]

5

Rocket City

1

Following the economic slump of the fifties and sixties, Rock Springs saw a meteoric energy boom in the late seventies. My parents, Stephanie and Jay, lived, met, and worked in Rock Springs during that time. They came of age in a place of extremes, a place where prostitution was openly accepted and everyone had cash; a place where you could get drive-thru liquor and any drug you wanted with ease.

As I listened to people tell me about this era, it made perfect sense that the town would capture the interest of Dan Rather and *60 Minutes*—and that there would be a murder as infamous as Sheriff Ed Cantrell shooting his deputy, Michael Rosa, not to mention the many other killings that occurred in Rock Springs. Considering the thrash-tempo recklessness of the era, those things seem inevitable. The following pages offer stories from people who moved to Rock Springs for what's now become its most notorious boom—and from those who watched their hometown mutate into something they no longer recognized.

STEPHANIE WESSEL ANSELMI: Rock Springs was fucking wild during the seventies.

JAY ANSELMI: The boom started not long after I graduated high school in 1975. I went to college in Laramie for a year, dropped out, and came back to Rock Springs in spring of 1976. There were a lot of good-paying jobs around here in the trona patch, and oil and gas was starting up pretty good. In the late seventies is when they had everything from K Street and the prostitutes. There were a lot of jobs, a lot of industrial work, and a lot of drugs. A guy could make just as much money around here with one of these jobs as he would if he had a college degree.

LES GEORGIS: Jim Bridger, the coal-fueled power plant and mine, came in and created some good jobs. The town moved up.

JACK SMITH: We went from a town of 10,000 people to a town of 30,000 people in what seemed like overnight.[1]

LISA SPANJERS: They'd charge a lot for rent in Rock Springs because of the demand. My apartment back in the seventies was $400 a month, which would've been enough to get a nice place in a city.

JUDY RODERICK: They were desperate back then. They lived anywhere they could. People would come knocking on your front door to ask if they could put a tent in your front yard.[2]

LES GEORGIS: When Union Pacific brought in Chinese laborers to bust the coal strike in the late 1800s, a lot of them lived in dugouts and ditches. The tent cities during the seventies were reminiscent of that.

NATE MARTIN: My mom is from North Dakota, and she was a teacher living in Minnesota. Her brother was an engineer, and he was helping to build a bridge in the Rock Springs area. He called my mom and told her about all the jobs there, that it was going through this huge boom. She ended up moving to Rock Springs and luckily found a house, even though there was a radical housing shortage. People were living in camps and caves. For her, it must've been a pretty wild experience. My dad talks about trying to date during that time, when the ratio of men to women was something like ten guys to one woman. My mom probably didn't think "Oh wow, ten guys to take your pick of" so much as she thought it was fucking gnarly. She got set up on a blind date with my dad.

TAMMY CURTIS MORLEY: I didn't find out about the real story of how my dad ended up in Rock Springs until his funeral.

I'm the fourth child out of five. My family is originally from Kansas. My mom's side is the good side. They're the ones who did the farming and lived life exactly how they were supposed to. They went to church every Sunday. My dad's side was more colorful. They lived in a nearby town. They had a farm, but they also had a nightclub. My dad ran moonshine. Years later, they escorted/kicked my dad out of the state of Kansas. He ended up in Nebraska, where he found work in the oil field. The company he worked for sent him to Rock Springs to see what was going on.

He was a gambler in addition to running moonshine. The story I got was that he went into the OK Corral bar, where he gambled with the Italians and Greeks. He came out with $7.50. This was in 1960, when I was two years old. He said, "Screw it. I'm going back in there." He came out with enough money to buy his own oil field water hauling truck. That's how our family ended up staying here.

During the boom, he ran a pool hall that was also a not-so-secret gambling parlor. My dad's name was Curly Curtis. His real name was L. J., but everyone called him Curly because of his hair. He would do his oil field thing during the day and run the pool hall at nighttime. The oil field guys would hang out and play pool and gamble upstairs.

LAURA: My parents came to Rock Springs from California in the seventies. My dad and his brother hopped on a train car in Sacramento and rode all the way to Rock Springs. They almost froze to death going over Donner Pass and a few other places in the mountains. They had nothing, no money or anything. They just wanted to get out of their situation in California.

Both of my parents grew up with several siblings in pretty intense poverty. So they wanted to go where the money was. My dad thought he could get a job in one of the mines, and that's what he ended up doing. He worked at Bridger Coal for twenty-five years. He was a dragline operator out there, which is a dangerous job. But he seemed like he always knew what was going on. He did some strip-mining-related work before Bridger as well, so he had a good career with that. And then my mom went to nursing school.

ROBERT B. RHODE: The Bridger mine was connected with the power plant by a seventy-foot-wide highway for the gigantic coal haulers that carried 110 tons in a single load at speeds of more than forty miles an hour. In 1977 the power plant consumed five million tons from a coal mine that could eventually be 4,000 feet wide and ten miles long.[3]

JAY ANSELMI: The first good-paying job I had was with Continental Emsco, which was an oil field warehouse job I had for about a year. People who needed oil field supplies would come in or they'd make an order, and we'd deliver it to their oil rig. Before that I worked construction for my uncle. I got paid five bucks an hour to carry cement. I helped build McDonald's, Imperial Apartments, and the Civic Center.

After Emsco, I started with Pacific Power and Light, which is the company that owned the Bridger plant and mine. I was twenty-three and worked as a maintenance helper for a few years, then as an ash disposal operator driving these seventy-five-ton trucks filled with coal ash. We'd dump the ash from the coal they burned in the plant. You'd work twelve-hour shifts. You had bottom ash and fly ash. The bottom ash wasn't too bad because it was more solid. The fly ash was like flour. You had to wear a respirator so you didn't breathe it in. It would blow everywhere in the wind and get real cute. One guy would drive and one guy would be in back to make sure you're in the right spot. You'd bang on the truck to tell them to stop or keep going. They'd have us rotate between day, swing, and graveyard shifts. Between the swing and graveyard, you'd only get a day and a half off. That could break you down if you didn't get good sleep.

There were all different kinds of people from all over who worked out there.

GINNY SPAIN: I was a nurse in Rock Springs, so I easily found jobs. I had a job at the nursing home just up from Hickory Street, and then a nurse position opened up out at Jim Bridger. I loved the job. It was all men, for one. That I liked immensely. I hardly remember any other women working there, except for just a few. It was also a very steady job. I made some good friends there, like this little cowboy guy who'd take me horseback riding. We'd ride horses and tie them up at the bar. We'd ride down the dirt road straight there.

I had to walk around all the job sites at the power plant and tell people to put their goggles on, stuff like that. A lot of times they didn't wear goggles. I also saw a lot of finger injuries. People would smash their nails, so I'd have to drill a hole in the nail to release the pressure. They'd drop stuff on their toes. Drilling through their nails was definitely not fun. I also saw a lot of burns, which was horrible because it would peel the skin off. With a burn on one guy's forearm, all the skin was rippled back. I had to take him into town because I couldn't handle it myself.

CHRIS SCHMIDT: My dad's dad moved their family to Rock Springs when my dad was sixteen or seventeen. This was during the seventies. My dad ended up dropping out of high school and joining the Navy within one year of living in Rock Springs. Moving into town as a sixteen-year-old, he didn't really find his stride until after the Navy. My mom has a pretty big family in McKinnon, Utah, which is right on the Utah/Wyoming border. The non–Native American side of my mom's family are Mormon and live in that area.

Half of my family identifies and is registered as Zuni, and the other half is Paiute Shoshone from Fallon, Nevada. My mom lived in Nevada and would go back and forth to another reservation to take care of my great-grandmother. When my mom was seventeen, she left the reservation and got a job as a nurse at the hospital in Rock Springs. That's when she and my dad met.

LISA SPANJERS: I met a boy in Minnesota that I ended up marrying, but he got back on drugs, and I moved back to California. He decided he was going to Rock Springs with a bunch of guys to make it rich during the boom. A bunch of them went together. I think there were eight of them.

When they were in Rock Springs, he started telling me that he misses me and still loves me, all this stuff—that he was going to come out and get me in California. We were both eighteen. He came out but didn't tell me he had a kilo of pot in the trunk. We got married in Vegas and ended up in Wyoming the next morning in a 1971 Pinto with no heat during the middle of winter. I remember driving into Wyoming and having to stop to scrape ice off the windows. We ended up living in a little trailer where all his friends also lived. He failed to mention before all this that there were ten guys to one girl in Rock Springs, and that's probably why he married me.

He didn't tell me about the pot until we got there. I'd never been to a town like it, and I had traveled a lot with my mom. How do you explain a place like Rock Springs? I called my mom after three days and told her I wanted to come home, that I'd made a mistake. But she told me to stick it out. My first idea to make money was that I'd sell pot. People were always coming over to the trailer.

My husband took me over to hang out with this couple he knew, and that was the first time I ever drank. I didn't like it at first and wanted to leave, but he wasn't being very cool about it. So I left, thinking he would come after me. He didn't. Three guys picked me up in a pickup. They were the nicest guys in the world. I couldn't remember what street we lived on, so these guys drove me around for two hours until we finally found the trailer.

JAY ANSELMI: The ratio of men to women was eleven to one, or something around there.

GINNY SPAIN: There were all these trailers full of guys who worked on the oil rigs. The high ratio of men to women was great for picking what you were interested in, that's for sure. And most of them were making good money. It could also get scary. There were bar fights; there were guns everywhere. You could just drive around with your shotgun or rifle in the back window. My husband had his in the back window. There were usually fights in the bars.

Anywhere there were a lot of men, there would be women looking. The guys would get off work and go to the bars, and every woman knew there were a lot of men at the bars. I actually didn't feel like anyone was preying on me or being threatening. Lots of flirting, though.

LISA SPANJERS: There were so many trailers where there'd be groups of guys from different places. You'd have six guys from Missouri, or six guys from Michigan, or wherever, and they'd all pack into these trailers. They'd live in the trailers, work in the oil field, and then, as soon as they had money, head back home. A lot of those workers came just to make money, and all they'd do was drink and party; or they'd put their heads down, focus on work, and send money to their families back home.

I eventually got a job working for Mountain Fuel and started making good money, too. Before that I was a maid at the Holiday Inn. My husband and I ended up getting a brand-new, fully furnished apartment right by the Holiday. It was outrageously nice, and we got it because my husband had connections with the Anselmis. I think it was your great-uncle who owned those apartments. We lived there until we bought our own trailer over on Blair Avenue, by the railroad tracks.

When I worked at the Holiday, there were a couple scary incidents. One of the other maids got raped in the hotel. That was it for me. So yeah, it was starting to get a little scary here and there. I was in some really crazy situations but somehow always came out unscathed.

STEPHANIE WESSEL ANSELMI: This one night, I'm not shitting you, we saw our friend—everyone called her Tex Ass—throw a guy right over a car. Just right over the top of it.

TAMMY CURTIS MORLEY: Shit yeah, I remember what it was like in Rock Springs during the seventies. There were a lot of places where my dad wouldn't let me work. Some of my friends worked at the A&W as carhops. My dad said absolutely not, because it was too dangerous. Two of my friends from high school were abducted from the A&W. One was put in the trunk, and one was raped.

I look back and feel thankful to my dad for not letting me do what all my friends were doing. We had a great time working at the answering service. You had to be able to handle a multitude of things. You had a switchboard, you had a phone. It was a good job.

My sister talks about what it was like going to school when Dad was sober. She was a little princess. When I was getting up to go to school, Dad was getting up to get his Crown Royal out of the cupboard. He gambled all night. My sister's and my life were totally different. Dad was working in the oil field when she grew up; he was at the pool hall when I was a kid.

ANDREA: I was around twenty-eight or twenty-nine at the time. I got married shortly after I moved to Rock Springs. There were a lot more men than women, but I was too busy working to get into the dating scene. My boss's husband told her to make sure I met someone so I wouldn't end up moving away. They had trouble finding someone who was good at running the beauty school—so when they found me, they didn't want me to get away. He said, "Find her a man to make sure she stays." He actually wanted to hook me up with Bill Anselmi because he was a bachelor, but I met my husband before that.

I left the beauty school to work in the salon at your grandpa's hotel, the Outlaw Inn. Then I injured my neck. My doctor told me I should find another occupation so I wouldn't hurt myself more. I went into bookkeeping and worked for an auto parts store. That's when I really found out that women were second-class citizens. I did bookkeeping, payroll, accounts receivable, accounts payable, invoicing, all of that. And then I found out the delivery guy was making more money than me. The boss just said he had a family to support. I guess the money I was making for my family was Monopoly money since my husband also worked. It hasn't gotten much better since then.

DANELLE: My mom's mom and her sisters moved here from Denver because their grandma moved here. My dad's family moved from Ogden, Utah. They moved here to work in the coal mines during the seventies boom. Being an African American family, racism is something we always dealt with in Rock Springs.

ORLANDO WEBB: I've seen that side of the town for sure. I've also seen people showing their better selves and not judging people by their race or ethnicity. It's definitely gone both ways, but I will say Rock Springs tends to have a blind eye toward that type of thing.

Most of my family has been here since before I was born. My great-grandfather and great-grandmother lived here, but some of my family has also come from other areas of the country. My mother and grandmother are from Memphis, Tennessee. My family is kind of a big stew of people from Rock Springs and people from other places. We've always been kind of a matriarchy.

My mom was a homemaker, and my dad worked in the mines, just like his dad and grandpa. Both he and my uncles worked at the power plant and the different mines. My dad was an underground crewman in the coal mines. He worked underground for most of his life. He's been injured by machinery, but it's just what he did. He got hit in the head one time and got some other bumps and bruises—nothing major, just the typical dangers of the job. He worked in the coal mines ever since he was eighteen up to when he retired, in his late fifties.

Those were the jobs being given out when he graduated high school. It was good money, benefits, and a way to take care of his family. We don't all necessarily get to do the job we love, or what we want to do all our lives. The attitude is that you appreciate the good-paying job that allows you to take care of your family. It was necessity and how he was raised, with his dad working in the mines.

JACK WATERS: I thought the people at the mines had it made. Where else could you make forty dollars an hour without a degree? I didn't make that much money working as an ICU nurse. And yet, I was the one who had to take care of you when you got in that mining accident.

JIMMY: I've lived through four booms. I remember the boom in the seventies when people were living in trailers and RVs right off the highway. It was nuts. You'd see a new kid at school every other week it seemed like, because people were constantly moving in.

People could really make a name for themselves during the big booms. There's a lot of people that came in during that seventies boom, stayed, and became very successful and well-known names in town. There are people who came in during the recent one, too, that have done really well.

I remember going to the New Grand Hotel as a kid, and there'd be hookers all up and down K Street. It was crazy as shit. I was only five or six.

TAMMY CURTIS MORLEY: I graduated in 1976, during the height of the prostitution that was in town. My dad told me horror stories so I would be careful. I used to walk around with keys between my fingers. You always had to check the back seat of the car before unlocking it. My friend Lucy and I would get a little wasted and go down to K Street to see all the action. It was right there, right in front of everybody's face. My dad's pool hall was right down there.

You would see the ladies of the night, and you'd see the pimps with their big coats. The girls were in all their glory. They had their high heels on, their coats, their nylon fishnets, their hair all done up, and they wore their dresses way high up. It was busy. There was a lot going on down there. I look back on it and think, "How did I live through that?"

My husband moved here during those times. We were in Bunning Park the other night listening to music, and he said, "My god, has this place ever changed." He talks about the A&D Saloon and how the girls used to come down there.

JAY ANSELMI: They had strippers at the A&D Saloon. There were a few times when I went into that bar and felt scared. I was always looking over my shoulder, especially when I went to the bathroom. The bar was one of a kind. The people when they'd get off work, they'd get a laugh and get into the activity there. You could get your wallet stolen or have someone do something else to you. I always tried to be really aware in there. The OK Corral bar was also popular in that area. You'd walk down K Street and get propositioned by prostitutes. There were a lot of heavy drugs around here: everything from marijuana to heroin, and everything in between.

The town had changed quite a bit from when I grew up. I'd never seen stuff like prostitution and illegal gambling before. Since there were so many high-paying jobs and guys with extra cash, I'm sure word got out, and that's why those things came into town. My friend got into one of the gambling halls when he was fourteen. He only had a few bucks on him when he went in, then he came out with this huge wad of cash. I'll never forget it. It was badass.

STEPHANIE WESSEL ANSELMI: I was seventeen when my family moved from Nebraska to the Rock Springs area. My mom managed a food service company, and my dad worked as a police officer in Lincoln. He was promised a promotion but didn't get it. My grandpa had purchased a building in Rock Springs and couldn't find reliable renters. The last one was a lush that couldn't run a business. The rumor about the renters was that they did too much coke and drank too much to keep things going. My mom and dad had always wanted to go into the restaurant business, so they upended everything to run a restaurant in the building Grandpa owned. Since Dad was a cop, he knew Rock Springs was pretty wild, with it being right off the interstate for the drug trade and the high ratio of men to women. I was seventeen and all up for moving out of Lincoln, Nebraska. This was 1977.

We moved during the summer, and when we got to Rock Springs, there was no housing available because of the boom. They couldn't build housing fast enough for the workers that were coming in. My parents finally found a shitty little double-wide near the Outlaw, and then three or four months later, they found a house to rent in Green River, fifteen minutes from Rock Springs. This whole time they were trying to build and establish their restaurant, White Mountain Mining.

I got a job at the Woolworth's on K Street. The Park Hotel was right there—that's where the sex workers would take their guys. All day long they would be walking back and forth in front of the store. The women would come in and buy things for their apartments. Most of the girls I met were very nice people.

At night, if you drove your car down K Street, you'd see sex workers everywhere and people partying. All the bars in that area were wild. There was an after-hours club owned by Earl Dotsey, where people could gamble. There were rumors that the owner was a pimp, which I think were partly true.

JACK WATERS: One of my dad's best customers was Earl Dotsey. We all called him Uncle Earl. He was the nicest guy in the world to us, but you knew not to screw with him.

JESSE REED: Earl Dotsey was my biological father, but I didn't know that until I was about sixteen or seventeen. It was crazy, man: he ran what they called an after-hours club that didn't open until two in the morning. That was right around the time I graduated high school. You had the prostitutes running all around town, and they'd hang out at my dad's club after the other bars closed. I just used to clean the place and go home.

There was lots of stuff going on: a lot of pimps and prostitutes walking down the street. But it was just a fact of life. My dad didn't talk to me a whole lot about the club. People were doing whatever they wanted back in those days. He died in 1980. He was irritated by the *60 Minutes* coverage, for sure, but he didn't say much about it to me.

J.J. ANSELMI: In 1977 Dan Rather and his TV crew came to town to cover the vice and corruption. They ended up doing two episodes about Rock Springs for *60 Minutes*. In the first one, they focus on Paul Wataha, the mayor at the time, who also worked as an accountant. He gets accused of cooking the books for Dotsey's club. The family who ran the pharmacy also say Wataha was embezzling, which they have proof of. I don't doubt any of that stuff was happening, but I do think there was this mundane, small-town aspect to that type of crime in Rock Springs, as well as the prostitution, that neither of those episodes touch on. I picture it as being similar to the early parts of *Boardwalk Empire*, where it was just this hometown, good ole boys club of backroom handshakes and cutting corners.

TAMMY CURTIS MORLEY: Wataha handled my dad's books. We went to church with his family. They were nice people. I'm sure they were only doing what they needed to help people in town survive. When I saw the *60 Minutes* with Wataha in it, I was sad to hear the man and woman who owned the pharmacy talk about how Wataha had embezzled money. I knew the woman, and she was a sweetheart.

JACK WATERS: When we ended up on *60 Minutes*, Dan Rather was on the front porch of my grandpa's house here. He was told to get the hell out of our town at that point.

J.J. ANSELMI: A cop in that first *60 Minutes* episode says that, when he tried to go to city council and Wataha about trying to get rid of the prostitution, he "was told to leave it alone." Dan Rather makes it seem so evil and unheard of, but that kind of thing, with town officials basically allowing prostitution to happen, is nothing new in mining towns in the West. It kept a lot of people out of jail who would've just gone back out to do the same shit.

I think the scarier part is how many more men than women there were, and what guys tend to do in those settings. The most terrifying part of that first *60 Minutes* episode is this night-vision footage of a guy getting upset with two sex workers. He moves at them like he's going to attack. They both pull out small knives and cut his face.

LES GEORGIS: I went to Texas and worked in the aerospace industry for about three years, until the Vietnam war wound down. I was working in Dallas when the *60 Minutes* episodes came out. All these guys came into my office and asked, "Is that the same Rocket City place where you're from?"

ANDREA: Our son was six years old during the boom. He always wanted to take a ride and show people K Street when they came to town. He'd say, "They have to see the hookers!" He would wave at all the girls on the street.

The women were mostly out during the night. We lived down on Ninth Street at the time, so we weren't very far from downtown. The scene down there didn't bother us much at all. We didn't see much of it because we weren't out much at night. We'd drive by the

Astro Lounge occasionally—but even then, if you hadn't heard it on the news, you wouldn't necessarily know what was going on.

A lot of the women came from Utah and Colorado. It was fast money for them. From that stretch by North Side State Bank down to the curve, that's where it was.

TAMMY CURTIS MORLEY: You couldn't miss it, with the girls walking up and down the street and the cars going back and forth. I have no idea where they all came from.

JESSE REED: The women came from all over the place. Some of them as far as the East Coast. Everyone heard about all the money from the coal and oil.

GINNY SPAIN: The sex workers on K Street looked pretty much like what you see on TV. They were scantily dressed, and they'd walk up to cars that would slow down or stop. But I didn't hang out in that scene much. I liked the Cowboy Bar a lot more.

JACK WATERS: It was rough and tough, but we had awesome schools, and we've always ranked high in the nation for outdoor activities. My mind is always kind of blown when people say there's nothing to do here. My friends and I used to ride our bikes down K Street to look at the pimps and sex workers. That was a game we played.

I thought it was a great place to grow up. I loved it and felt lucky to not be from one of the families that were coming in, who didn't know anyone. I had a big support system of family here. I knew about the drugs and prostitution and all the gambling that went down at places like the OK Corral. None of that was a shock to me.

TAMMY CURTIS MORLEY: I actually think the prostitution was kind of a good thing. There could have been a lot more crime; it took care of a big part of the male population here. There were probably less assaults and kidnappings because of it.

DUDLEY GARDNER: *60 Minutes* came to town and sensationalized the prostitution and gambling. For a lot of the old timers, it was upsetting. Prostitution had been here for decades, just like it was in other mining towns. It was something they didn't necessarily see as a social evil, just as long as it stayed within one section of town. There was a separation between prostitution and everyday life. People in town didn't see it as something shameful until *60 Minutes* came along. There are multiple places in the world, such as New Zealand, that have had a similar approach. It's part of the bigger picture. But after outsiders came in and looked down on it, people felt ashamed. They didn't want to be looked down upon.

J.J. ANSELMI: After the *60 Minutes* episodes aired, there was political pressure on the cops and local government to clean things up.

TAMMY CURTIS MORLEY: When my niece was two years old, she and her family lived in an apartment behind the pool hall. You could see the pool hall from the window. She watched the feds come in and bust people for gambling in the backroom. The gambling was just a bunch of old guys who were trying to get out of their wives' hair. I worked there cleaning up, and I remember how the old guys would spit; it would never get in the damn toilet.

I worked the night the feds came, but I'd already left. I already made my gas money for the night. Apparently the feds came in and told the Rock Springs cops they didn't have a choice: they had to make the gambling bust at the pool hall. They arrested all these older men. My dad asked if they could at least not put handcuffs on the older people. I knew one of the cops, old man Callas, who made the bust. He told me that he had a younger officer on the force go in ahead of him so he didn't have to arrest his own brother, who was in there gambling. He saw his truck out front when they pulled up.

Callas was one of the two cops who were there when Cantrell shot the other cop, Rosa. That whole thing was a devastation. I used to hang out with Cantrell's daughter. I'd go over to their house. Her mom was a doll. Her older brother died when they lived in Lusk, Wyoming—I think it was in a car wreck. She said that ever since her brother died, her dad wasn't the same. He'd walk in the house and not even acknowledge her. I only knew Cantrell as this stone-faced dude. Years later, the daughter got pregnant, and I remember her telling me that her dad didn't even notice.

JIMMY: When Cantrell shot Rosa, that was really a big moment for the town.

GINNY SPAIN: I clearly remember when Cantrell shot Rosa in the parking lot. That was . . . Jesus.

J.J. ANSELMI: Cantrell murdering Rosa is the most well-known Rock Springs story from this era, for sure. A&E did a special on it, and there was an essay about it in *Harper's*. It also got coverage in the *New York Times* and some other big newspapers.

Cantrell was brought in as sheriff to clean up the town after the *60 Minutes* episodes aired—and then he hired Rosa, who was originally from New York, because he had more undercover experience than the local cops. At some point, things soured between them; there was some chest-puffing and threats. There was a state investigation looking into corruption in the Rock Springs police force, and Rosa was subpoenaed to testify. Cantrell shot Rosa in a parked car just a few nights before Rosa's testimony. There are lots of theories about that, everything from it being a coincidence to people who think Rosa had uncovered something big about the RS police and was about to drop a testimonial bomb. There were two other cops in the car: Bider and Callas. The murder was a tragedy for lots of reasons. Rosa had kids and a wife. He abused women, but he was still a dad.

Cantrell ended up getting exonerated based on a self-defense argument by his lawyer, Gerry Spence. It's mind-blowing to think Spence made that case by highlighting what a quick draw Cantrell was. From there, he said Cantrell saw Rosa reach for his gun and was able to shoot him first, even though Rosa hadn't gotten his gun out. It's worth noting that Rosa was Black and Puerto Rican, so maybe getting an all-white jury in Wyoming to exonerate a white cop for murdering a person of color wasn't surprising at all.

JAY ANSELMI: If I remember right, that's when Mr. Ed Cantrell shot Mr. Rosa, who was an undercover narcotics agent. He shot him in the back of the cop car when they were in the parking lot of the Silver Dollar Bar, across from the Outlaw Inn. I always heard, but don't know how true it is, that Rosa was one of those undercover narcotics agents who would bust people and then keep some of the drugs. Instead of turning them in, he would resell the drugs. This is just what I heard, but I think it might be true. I heard it from people in other small towns, too, where Rosa might've been selling cocaine and marijuana. So basically he was double-dipping and making money that way.

Years later, I'd see Ed Cantrell in his yard when I was meter reading.

JACK WATERS: As a young medical worker, I was actually on the call—the big call—at the Silver Dollar, if you know what I'm talking about. I was on the Michael Rosa call when I was fifteen. I ended up testifying about it. I was right in the middle of it. There were a lot of weird details about that night that, looking back, seem suspicious. The other two cops besides Cantrell had their regular guns and then sidearms on their calves, like they went there ready for something to happen. The tension in that car must've been incredible. You have to wonder, what was Rosa going to say about the Rock Springs Police Department in his testimony?

CHRIS HAWKS: Around 1979 or 1980, my stepdad, Gerry Spence, was the special prosecutor in a murder case in Evanston, Wyoming. This guy, Mark Hopkinson, had been accused of blowing up the county attorney's house and killing him, his wife, and one of his kids, and also of torturing one of the key witnesses in the case to death. I knew the witness. Hopkinson had made death threats against my stepdad and my family while this prosecution was taking place. We had twenty-four-hour police security for months. It was during that summer that the Cantrell thing went down in Rock Springs. Cantrell called my stepdad to represent him. My mom was like, "There's no fucking way you're representing that guy." And Gerry said, "This is what I do. I'm going to meet with him."

I remember Cantrell coming to the ranch with his son, Joe, who had this really sick black Camaro. It was surreal because we had all this security detail and the stuff going on with Hopkinson—and here was this cop who pulled up and had been accused of murdering one of his own. Gerry not only agreed to defend Cantrell, but almost immediately he made Cantrell the chief of his security detail during the Hopkinson trial. So you had this dynamic of this cop who'd killed another cop all of a sudden being the lead for all these other cops at the ranch.

That summer, Cantrell took me under his wing. If I was awake, I was with the guy. He taught me everything I know about guns, and he was a phenomenal mentor to me. He was a small guy but very fit. He was barrel-chested, quiet, and had these piercing blue eyes. He didn't say a whole lot, but when he spoke, he spoke with purpose. Even as a mentor, he didn't say much. He mentored more through his actions. Ed had a son who died, and we probably talked about that more than anything. It haunted him for his whole life.

I spent hours and hours and days and days on horseback with him because we were living on a cattle ranch. You're constantly out on horseback when you're on a cattle ranch, moving cattle around between grazing sections and checking on them. You're riding the range. He definitely helped me grow up. We would spend all day at the gun range on the ranch. I think he really appreciated that: even though he was facing a first-degree murder charge, my folks fully entrusted him with me. I don't remember him talking about the charge much, but I remember feeling very scared for him when the trial came around.

The trial was in Pinedale. I remember leaving school and staying in a motel and going to court every day. I was thirteen years old, and I remember the jury coming in and reading the verdict like it was yesterday. I literally broke down and cried because I was so relieved Ed wasn't going to prison. A reporter asked Cantrell if he had any comments. He just said, "Fuck 'em. I'm free." My stepdad had that quote framed in his office. After that, I lost track of Ed for a long time. He sort of disappeared after the trial, but I know he went through some hard times.

DUDLEY GARDNER: I knew the prosecuting attorney in the Cantrell case. He was one of my students. He felt like there were a lot of politics present in that case—and there was no way he could convict Cantrell of first-degree murder. He was outmanned and out-financed.

There were some locals who didn't like the outside interference in the case. They thought it should be handled within the town. That libertarian way of thinking is still very strong in Rock Springs.

ANDREA: I was up in Sheridan for a class reunion when Cantrell shot Rosa. We heard it on the radio. People started talking about Rock Springs as such a troubled place. I remember thinking, "Are we talking about the same town?" I mean yeah, the prostitutes were there, but we didn't see them unless we went looking.

JIMMY: [There was also another murder]—Harlow murdered Tammy Schoopman during the seventies boom. I actually got a ride from that dude. He was on the track team, believe it or not, and he was a decent athlete. He gave me and my friend a ride after school about a year after he killed Schoopman. They ended up finding Tammy's body in the dumpster next to the woodshop at the high school.

That was scarier than shit. He didn't get caught for that murder for quite a while. He'd already killed her when he gave me and my friend a ride. He didn't get caught until he tried to stab a guy about a year later. The guy got away, and Harlow confessed to the Schoopman murder when he was being questioned about that other stabbing. Harlow is still alive and ended up killing a guard in prison.

I also knew that guy, Robertson, who killed the old lady. He lived right by my grandparents' house and would ride his bike through the alley. My grandpa and I would shoot basketball in the driveway and sometimes Robertson would join us—or he would throw a handful of gravel at us and giggle. He was nuts, kind of the neighborhood punk. I would hang out at his house with his sister when we were kids. He was very strange. You could see trouble there. My guess would be that he got picked on quite a bit, because that stuff can wear on people. Rock Springs can be a little rough on outsiders. Certain kids can get away with doing that to people.

Robertson was seventeen or eighteen when he snuck into the woman's house and shoved a knife in her throat. I'm not sure why he did it. I think she'd yelled at him years earlier to get off her sidewalk when he was walking home from school. There were a lot of older people in that area who didn't want you messing with their fence or going near their yard. That was before they tore down all those houses on Dewar Drive. It's kind of fucked up to look back and think I went to school with two murderers.

DUDLEY GARDNER: There were more people murdered in Rock Springs the first year I was there than the entire time I lived in Craig, Colorado. It was a shock to my system that there were so many deaths in such a short amount of time. I'm a Vietnam veteran and wasn't naïve. The violence in Rock Springs was shocking. That part has gotten much better, but the town is still dealing with drugs, alcoholism, and suicide.

JAY ANSELMI: A guy shot one of my best friends, Jim Richmond, in the early eighties. I was one of his pallbearers. It happened over at Gaviotis' late in the night. Jim was four years older than me, and he got shot the night before he turned thirty. He always tried to break up fights. He was a brown belt in karate and didn't like to see people fight. He always felt that, even if he didn't know people, he'd rather not see them fight.

He was around the wrong people one night. Him and two other guys got into it. One guy got shot twice and is lucky to be alive, but Jim got shot and died. The guy who shot them was a coke dealer, so I think something else was going on there. He's in prison. He tried to escape, but he got caught and they gave him even more time. At Jim's funeral, his mother told me she had a dream a long time before that her son would get killed the night before he turned thirty.

2

DUDLEY GARDNER: Plenty of bootleggers used to live in Rock Springs during Prohibition. In the seventies, that smile-and-wink culture continued on with drugs.

TAMMY CURTIS MORLEY: I partied hard during the seventies. There were a lot of drugs in Rock Springs. My friend's brother used to take cash from their family's business to the bank. He popped his head into a shop and got shot. He was twelve. His parents believed he walked into a drug deal gone bad. He saw something he shouldn't have.

JAY ANSELMI: It's all a spider web around here with how everyone is connected.

J.J. ANSELMI: A week after that first *60 Minutes* episode about the mayor and corruption aired, they put one out about my grandpa, Don Anselmi, who owned the Outlaw Inn, and his alleged connections to organized crime. The main accusation is that Grandpa Don got the district attorney to wipe an arrest off his business partner's son's record. The dude was just a low-level weed dealer. Rather also alleges that my grandpa was connected to land scandal people in Arizona and "mobsters." There's no real proof in the episode, so who knows? I'm waiting for the FBI to send me Grandpa Don's file, but it takes three years or more. Hopefully I can find out for sure. Either way, everyone in town thought the Anselmis were in the mafia after the second *60 Minutes* episode came out. I've also heard rumors that Bill, Don's brother, was doing some trafficking out of his furniture store. Uncle Bill shot himself about twelve years later, although some people in our family think he was murdered.

LISA SPANJERS: My husband got a job at Bill Anselmi's furniture store as the warehouse manager. That's how I got into the shady side of Rock Springs. Plus my husband was getting back on drugs and drinking a lot. We all started partying a lot. Pretty soon I was full blown into drinking, pot, you name it. It wouldn't surprise me if there was some illegal stuff happening at the warehouse where my husband worked. Him and his coworker were pretty heavy into the drug scene.

I remember Bill getting married to this really beautiful woman. He was heavyset, always sweating, had bad manners, and was just kind of gross. But here he comes with this bombshell woman. He was so generous with us. He floated our entire vacation to Mazatlán, all expenses paid. Bill held a contest with a Ford Fiesta where the last person with their hand on it got to keep it. It lasted three days. I'm pretty sure my husband was in the bathroom the whole time, snorting lines. Bill paid for so much for us. When I met him, he was like God, you know?

My ex would deliver a lot of furniture for Bill up to Jackson, so we got to stay at his house up there. It was such a glorious house. The blinds were remote-controlled. I remember thinking it was the most high-tech thing I'd ever seen. He also had this crazy bar. Everything was shaped in a U, even the furniture. He had it decked out. For the location, I bet it would be worth ten million today.

GINNY SPAIN: We'd close out the bars and then go over to Bill Anselmi's place to finish out the night. We were doing whatever. I never did heroin, but we did a lot of pot, mushrooms, and acid, and we all drank like fish. I loved hallucinogens when I was drinking. Mushrooms were the funnest.

One night, I slept outside under a bridge. I got in a fight with my husband. I was flirting or chatting with another gentleman in the bar. My husband got pissed and told me I couldn't come home. Instead of going somewhere else, I decided to walk down the railroad tracks. I found a bridge and just kind of curled up there. People wonder why there were so many killings and people found dead. God must've been keeping an eye on me or something, because there were many times I could've not been here anymore. I made a lot of poor decisions back then, and the alcohol didn't help. That's what happens to your noggin when you're frying it on a daily basis: you get a little crazy.

My husband and I would put a bottle away between us when we partied. It was amazing. Everyone was partying. I wouldn't encourage my kids to do it, but I'm glad I did.

KARA: My dad partook in what the town had to offer at the time, which was a lot of drinking and partying. He contracted hepatitis C but didn't know it until about thirty years later. The doctor told him he got it during the seventies. When he was going through chemo later in life, he'd joke that he'd been training his body to handle the chemicals since he was a teenager.

ANDREA: When I first moved to Rock Springs, my boss got me an apartment on C Street, next door to the Pacific Market. There were four rooms in there. The first night I got to town, I unloaded my car and went to sleep. This terrible noise woke me up. I went back to sleep, but the next morning, as I was eating breakfast, I heard the sound again. It was my neighbor retching in the toilet. The walls were paper-thin. He'd gone out on a bender the night before. That was my first night in Rock Springs.

LISA SPANJERS: I was pretty awful, especially after I separated from Dick. Line dancing was big at the time, and I was out constantly. I actually hate country music but just liked the dancing. I had my cowboy boots and everything. We'd go out to the cowboy bars. I met this great guy named Clyde, whose dad was the principal of the high school. But I cheated on him all the time. He was going to school at the community college and working as a janitor at night, and I was out partying. There was so much temptation because, once I got to drinking, I always had my pick of any guy I wanted to go home with. I would just go approach guys I thought were hot, and I did that quite a bit.

I ended up regretting it quite a bit. I slept with my boyfriend's best friend while he was on vacation in Florida. We both felt so guilty that we had to tell him. He was such a nice guy and forgave me. I felt too horrible and had to leave him, though. He ended up moving to Utah and starting a successful chiropractic practice. I had a dream about him one night; he told me not to worry about past mistakes. I woke up the next day and found his eulogy. I have this weird psychic connection with the people I met in Rock Springs.

JESSE REED: There were a lot of dirt roads going through town, a lot of railroad tracks and shit. We used to drive the drag and park over by Ace. Cops would drive right behind you and not even do anything, even though they knew you were drinking. You'd drive from one end of Rock Springs to the other and pick up mixed drinks along the way and anything else you wanted. You'd grab a drink in the drive-thru and just keep on going.

STEPHANIE WESSEL ANSELMI: You could drive through Chuck's, and if you were a pretty girl, they'd give you free drinks to go. We were just giggling schoolgirls. We'd pull up to the window and order tequila sunrises, and they'd give them to us in plastic cups for free. I had a fake ID, which my boyfriend at the time doctored. Women could get into the bars without getting carded anyway. They were so happy to have a pretty girl in there. At the time, I didn't know enough for it to be scary. My friends and I would go to the bars and dance all night and then just go home. I couldn't hold my liquor, so I didn't get that drunk. Then I always drove home.

You could get drinks to go at all the bars. Everyone in town was driving drunk all the time. People didn't really talk about not doing it. There were fights, but I was usually home by the time the fights broke out. I remember playing tennis near the high school, where there was this wall commemorating all the students who'd died in automobile accidents. Drunk driving was involved in a lot of those deaths, for sure. The drinking age back then was only eighteen or nineteen.

JIMMY: My dad died at work when I was seven, so I kind of understood death from an early age. My mom's brother, who helped me get through my dad's death, died a year and a half later in a car wreck. Him and this guy he was drinking with at a bar hit each other over on the belt loop, head on.

My dad worked for Tom's Wyoming Glass. He had a Purple Heart from Vietnam. Great dude. He was doing a job out in Point of Rocks. On his way home, this truck driver dozed off on the interstate [and hit my dad's car]. That was April 18, 1979. They didn't have seatbelts back then. He got thrown from the truck. So I came home from school to find out my dad died. All that made me an atheist almost immediately. We weren't a big church family anyway. I was only a kid, but I was like, "Man, I don't know about all this," with the church stuff.

GINNY SPAIN: There was a liquor store right by the power plant, so we'd stop there to get a couple to-go drinks for the way home because it was about twenty-five miles back to Rock Springs. It was actually very convenient.

LISA SPANJERS: We used to spend a lot of time up in Sheep Creek Canyon, which is right on the Wyoming/Utah border. We'd get these huge groups to go out there and party. After a while, I got to know the caves so well that I would be the person to bring people out. You're hiking miles and miles up this mountain to get there. The second you came back over the Wyoming border from Utah, there was this bar, and it was our favorite place. We'd get shit-faced and drive the hour-plus drive back home.

We used to get these drinks called Squeezos, which was just grenadine and Everclear. They'd hand them to us right out the window of the drive-up liquor stores. We were always drinking and driving. There were also guns in the back windows. That was the norm in that time and place.

We used to go to the Flaming Gorge dam a lot, too. Everything always involved booze. I don't remember doing anything without it being around. For any occasion, we had booze along. I've always been a big pot smoker, too. We always had weed.

JIMMY: I had some Italian buddies who could buy booze when they were in ninth grade. They had five o'clock shadows by four o'clock. The drinking age was nineteen back then. We were the last state in the union to change it to twenty-one. Driving drunk was kind of a rite of passage.

TAMMY CURTIS MORLEY: There was one night I was out drinking with my friends and just doing the normal Rock Springs thing. I was driving, and we were coming back from a big party out at Arnoldi's. I got picked up by a sheriff. He asked me to blow in his face to check my breath. I remember the wind was blowing. He looked at my license and asked if I was Curly's daughter. I said I was, and he said, "Tell him I say hello," then he let us go. That was a normal thing in Rock Springs. When I told my dad the next morning, he laughed. It was the way things were. I just assumed my dad paid the cops off. Cops used to hang out down at the pool hall.

STEPHANIE WESSEL ANSELMI: Our family restaurant got started on a shoestring, making the money for improvements with bar sales. Every piece of equipment was a big deal to buy. Dad remodeled the inside with salvaged barnwood. One of the movie theatres was remodeling and tore out all their carpet. My parents bought it, and we pieced together the carpet on the floor by sewing it up. You'd use this big carpet needle to sew the carpet to the floor.

Once my parents' place was going more, I quit my job at the Holiday to work there. I knew how to bartend even though I wasn't of age, and soon we started cleaning up. I took accounting classes at the community college and did all the books. My sisters, who were four and five years younger than me, would wash dishes. We all worked so hard. We had to put food on the table.

The boom was in full swing at this point. We would turn over two or three times a night. On Friday and Saturday nights, you'd get to the point at the bar where you had to turn people away. In addition to everything else he did, my dad would stand at the jukebox and bounce, kicking people out if they got too drunk or rowdy. Since he'd been a police officer, Dad was really good at getting people out. The guys in the bands would help him if he needed it. One night, he had to throw someone out and things got ugly. I was worried, so I opened up the side door to make sure he was okay. I'm not shitting you: this guy was standing there, and your grandpa slugged him so hard the guy flew through the air—but his shoes stayed on the ground, just sitting there. I'd never even seen a fight before. It was like moving into the *Twilight Zone*.

There was another time when he had trouble kicking out these two brothers. He finally got them out the door—but I was worried, so I went out there and these two guys have my dad in the corner, and they're both hitting him. I turned around and grabbed this little cocktail glass and started hitting one of the guys in the head with it. The glass broke in my hand, and after it was done breaking, I ground the glass into his head, turning my hand side to side. I had so much adrenaline. His head and hair was all bloody, then they finally left.

I had this huge gash in my hand. I ended up cutting my tendons and index finger. Because of the boom, the hospital had this renowned hand surgeon. He reattached my tendon, which was a novel procedure at the time. I was about twenty. It was a regular thing to have to throw people out. Things would get violent.

Not long after that, I was out of town, and it was a school night for my sisters, so it was just Mom and Dad working. There was this family in the area who were known for getting in fights and just tearing the hell out of bars. They jumped my parents. It still makes me cry to think about it. The next day, my mom had a black eye from getting beat up. I was so shocked: they hit my mom.

I think my parents ended up biting off more than they could chew. They were both professional people, but this place was so goddamn wild. They'd walked into this hard, crusty, blue-collar party life. With jobs in the coal mines, oil field, and trona mines, there really was a lot of money there. Everyone had cash. It was also during the time when people used cocaine recreationally. No one talked about it being addictive. So you'd get coke when you'd go out and party, and everyone would do some and then go home. But of course that turned into something really ugly. It was accepted at the time, though. It wasn't weird to walk into the bathroom and see everyone putting little spoons up to their nose. Through all that, my parents kept running their restaurant. They did eventually make enough money to build their own house.

TAMMY CURTIS MORLEY: My first husband was really a Jekyll-and-Hyde character. He was one of the best dudes you could ever be around from grade school up. I fell in love with him. He was a great guy. But things changed when he got into drugs. I remember when he fell and got injured. We couldn't keep any pain pills in the house or anything like that. I didn't know the guy he turned into. He was using and abusing. The things he said, the things he did—I had to write it in a journal and cut my ties with him to work myself up to get a divorce. The worst Christmas of my life was with him. It was horrible.

LISA SPANJERS: I'll never know exactly what happened to my husband. I don't think it was suicide, even though that's what some people believed. I talked to him earlier that evening, but he kept on partying. I don't know what happened, or how his trailer caught on fire. His friends were shady, too. We lived a block away from each other and would see each other at the bars. We were talking about getting back together right before the end.

When Dick died in Rock Springs, he was burnt to nothing. He talked to me that night because it was our anniversary. I pretty much told him to fuck off. One of his best friends was a fireman. He had to see him like that. There was this little chocolate lab locked in the back room that survived. I've always felt guilty.

Before that, Dick had gotten another girl from Minnesota to come marry him in Rock Springs. Her name's Ginny Spain, and we've become great friends over the years. She ended up having Dick's kid. She was interrogated about the fire because they thought it was shady and might've been started by someone.

GINNY SPAIN: My husband and I got in a bad fight, so I moved back to Minnesota with my baby. That's when that fire happened in his trailer and he died. I actually don't think it was an accident, either. I think someone killed him, although I'm not sure who. The FBI called me at one point to ask me about him—what he was up to, and who he knew—so I know for a fact they were looking into it. It makes no sense to me that he'd leave something on the burner, or that he'd run back in the burning trailer to get his dog. None of it fits together in my head. There were for sure murders and killings in Rock Springs. The FBI had been looking into him for selling drugs.

I would've settled down in Rock Springs if my husband hadn't died. You didn't have to go to the bars. It's beautiful out there. There was fishing, hunting, and all sorts of things to do outdoors.

LISA SPANJERS: For me, Rock Springs had started to become home. Back then, a lot of people that came into town for the boom didn't find the true gold and beauty of Wyoming that I did by really getting to know people from there. People who'd grown up there showed me everything. We traveled through the state.

I probably wouldn't have left if my ex hadn't gotten killed. I'd also just had that abortion. It was a bad situation, so I thought I'd move back to Minnesota and go to college. But I did see most of the out-of-town people as being temporary, whereas I'd made Rock Springs a home.

My ex's best friend became the head of BLM, plus he was in the fire department. He made bank. He was able to retire in his late fifties. Same thing with another of my friends who worked at Mountain Fuel. She retired at fifty-eight. She's set for life. Had I played my cards right, I would've made money and left there a lot differently than I did.

ROBERT B. RHODE: While the rest of the nation slid into a mild recession, the Rock Springs boom simply collapsed . . . Trona production began a serious plunge in mid-1982 primarily because of a decline in the demand for new glass . . . A second contributor to the recession in Rock Springs was the drying up of the oil patch.[4]

TAMMY CURTIS MORLEY: It seemed to me like the boom left all at once. The town was dead. The oil fields dried up. All the rest just went away.

ROBERT B. RHODE: The recession punctured the demand for electrical power as well, and as a result the Bridger plant was operated in 1983 at one-half capacity . . . and this resulted in layoffs at the coal mine.[5]

LES GEORGIS: When jobs at the power plant started to go away, all the construction and tent cities went away.

DUDLEY GARDNER: Everyone started moving out when the boom busted. There wasn't a reckoning with how quickly that had come and gone. I'll never forget how a local historian put it. "We didn't believe the boom would come," she said. "And when it was here, we didn't believe it would ever leave." There was no preparation.

JACK WATERS: The problem I had with the boom was you had all these people and companies move in who just took when they left. We were left to pick up the pieces while they walked out of here with cash up the wazoo. It was a lot of, "Oh well, we don't care about this place. We're only here for the jobs." All the things we as taxpayers had funded throughout the boom—we were still saddled with those expenses when the town went into bust.

6

At Least We Have Each Other

Times of extreme prosperity and debauchery always meet some type of reckoning. For Rock Springs's biggest boom, reckoning came in the form of a stark bust that lasted for the better part of two decades. Workers and companies ditched town as if the air was poisonous. For the people who survived that era, it was most often because their friends, family, and neighbors were there to help them through. But even community couldn't stop despair from taking hold.

The suicide rate skyrocketed. The town's penchant for wild partying started to look a lot more like widespread addiction. Without as many high-paying jobs, it became harder for residents to cope with the relentless wind and unforgiving winters. Rock Springs during the late seventies was the beautiful person on those optical illusion drawings that become something else when flipped upside-down. The town during the eighties was the ugly side of the illusion.

LAURA: There's something called Gillette Syndrome, which states that these pop-up mineral extraction communities get these rushes of people who don't stick around or get absorbed into the community. They end up leaving—but you have all these structures that were built to sustain them. So you end up with these bare-bones communities that are sucked dry, like Rock Springs and Gillette. There were always abandoned structures and pieces of mining communities on the edges of town that people left because they weren't sustainable. That really changes the atmosphere.

ASHLEY: You have a bunch of people who come to Rock Springs to make fast money in one of the industries, whether it's trona, oil, or coal. But then when that money isn't coming in, it puts a lot of stress on people. There's nothing else here to make that much money. There's nowhere to turn.

STACY: When I was growing up, the Rock Springs economy was on its way down. The boom-and-bust cycle is hard on people. I always think back to our high school theater, which could seat four or five hundred people. It had a hydraulic orchestra pit, which was fairly unheard of in a coal mining town. So money would get poured into infrastructure during boom periods, but then you have these bust periods when people are hard up for luck and the infrastructure deteriorates and doesn't get maintained. What you'll see are these relics of what the town used to be—but it's not like that anymore, and that can be depressing and devastating for the fabric of the community. You also see a steep population decline.

JACK WATERS: By the time the eighties came, I was used to the boom-and-bust cycle. It was just, "Here we go again." For me, it always returned back to old Rock Springs. The majority of people that stayed had been here before the boom started. They were here when we went into the bust. That makes everyone come together, even if your opinions are different.

DUDLEY GARDNER: I think the eighties bust was about as tough a time as you could ever live through in Wyoming. It looks like it might be getting that way [again] now.

The community college promised me that I'd get steady raises every year. Ten years later, the bust hit. One of the biggest moments of growth I've had in my life was surviving that bust. My trailer burned down in 1983. I lost everything I owned.

I didn't have any resources to get a new trailer or a new place. This is when I fell in love with Rock Springs. The school put me in a house, rent-free. People from the community brought me everything I needed. When I got my own house in 1989, they gave it to me for such a low price. My book, *Forgotten Frontier*, had just come out, but here I was with no money. Rock Springs took care of me. They wanted me to stay. The bankers in town were also good to me because I was documenting the community's history.

LES GEORGIS: When you live through an economic collapse like that, the devastation on people is incredible. Rock Springs, and Wyoming in general, has a high rate of alcoholism. They talk about the wind, depression, and lots of things in connection with that. Economics causes some of it, too. The bars were always full when I was a kid. If the mines were empty, the bars were full.

JIMMY: I used to work for my stepdad, who was a homebuilder. I probably built between twenty-five and thirty houses in Rock Springs. Someone would get a twelve pack of Mickey's or a case of Pabst, and we'd drink with the concrete guys at the end of the day. It was a reward for busting your ass all day. Tons of dudes drink two or three beers a night and keep it there, but then it turns into a drinking issue for a lot of people. I personally haven't had a drink in four years. I didn't have a huge problem, but it's definitely been a nemesis in my life.

KARA: A lot of the drinking seemed antisocial in Rock Springs, a way to escape and turn further inward.

LAURA: For the generation just before mine, it didn't seem like anyone was telling them "no." In Rock Springs, there was almost a competition with how much you could do or abuse as far as drugs and alcohol. There was a weird competitive streak that's still there. People want to be the most intense, the person who does more, so there's a lot of escalation. I remember people in high school saying stuff like, "My god, did you see how much he drank this weekend, or how much pot she smoked?" Volume was important to people to keep your street cred.

LES GEORGIS: It can be a tragedy to watch alcoholism pass through families, from generation to generation. My good friend was building his house in Rock Springs, and he was living in a trailer in the garage while he was doing it. I went over there and stayed a few days to help him. That's when I found out how bad things had gotten. I'm amazed he lived as long as he did. We'd get up and eat breakfast, and he'd drink a full water glass with straight gin. He had one in his hand all day. He still built the house beautifully. He was the highest functioning alcoholic I've ever seen. He didn't do that well in school, but he was highly intelligent. The house was built in a very efficient way. They paid next to nothing for electricity.

JAY ANSELMI: People started to get a bad attitude because we were trying to get the same work done at the power plant, but with almost half the workers gone.

STEPHANIE WESSEL ANSELMI: During one of your dad's first jobs, he walked into the warehouse and found the owner's body. He'd hung himself. He was an intravenous drug user. Someone from the next generation in that family died by suicide, too.

I think there's a high rate of mental illness and depression in Rock Springs. But there were no mental health resources for people. We knew lots of people who got hardcore into drugs.

My uncle-in-law shot himself in the eighties. He'd been through multiple booms and busts in Rock Springs, working in the car business. He'd started over several times, watching each of his businesses fail. When you buy cars, they give you a certain amount of inventory, and you have to move it to get more. He'd built this huge car lot, but things were falling apart. The guys from GMC were coming to town, and his inventory wasn't going to square. His wife, who was addicted to pain pills, was also having an affair. She was beautiful but always kind of out of it. I think it was all those things coming together when he shot himself.

J.J. ANSELMI: My great-uncle Bill killed himself when I was four, but I have very little recollection of him or that time. My dad has always thought he was murdered. I guess Uncle Billy really took to me and asked my parents if he could adopt me. He never had kids of his own.

JACK WATERS: I was working at the hospital when your great-uncle shot himself. I've seen a lot of suicide, especially since I've spent so much time working in the emergency room. The first time I remember a family member dying by suicide was my uncle—his wife and my mom were essentially raised as sisters. He ended up killing himself because his wife died. He couldn't deal with it.

My little brother had always taken care of my mom and dad. When my dad died, he lived at my mom's house and took care of her. He gave up his entire life to take care of Mom. When she died, he had nothing. It got to the point where he couldn't deal with it. I think that's the biggest thing: it can be a hell place to live if you're by yourself. He'd lost his job, and it wasn't easy for him to find another. He had the three biggest stressors in life: losing your house, getting a divorce, and losing your job. So then you kill yourself.

DUDLEY GARDNER: I do think the suicide rate is connected to the boom-bust cycle. I also think it connects to expectations of success people impose on themselves. They don't forgive themselves when they don't live up to those expectations. People experience a lot of shame when they lose a job, or when their finances aren't good. And they're much more likely to kill themselves if they don't have a support system.

There are people in Rock Springs and across the country in great pain, people who can't get jobs, who don't see a bright future. Sometimes they start to feel that, no matter what steps they take, they won't be able to move forward. Social dislocation and economic stress are very present in Rock Springs. People self-medicate with drugs and alcohol, or they might end up taking that most desperate step, which is killing themselves.

TAMMY CURTIS MORLEY: I used to get angry just wondering why there's so much suicide here. There was a kid in my class who killed himself, in part because of the shame he felt for being gay. Think about it. It was 1976 in Wyoming. He was such a kind person. What would he be doing now if he was still here?

JIMMY: I was looking at an old junior high yearbook, and there's this group of four kids whose pictures all touch who all died. Three of them killed themselves. The fourth kid got killed up on White Mountain. In addition to that, I've had four good friends who killed themselves. Some people don't do it in one day. They do it over a period of time, where they party so hard every day and live their life on the edge.

It's shit work, wind, the bitter cold. I'd be interested to know what's the worst month for suicides here, because goddamn, February is a tough month to get through. It's the shortest month—but man, that can be the hardest one. A lot of people also get in financial trouble. They might spend their money on expensive toys and find themselves in all this debt. So there can be a lot of stress to make payments on anything from your car, house, boat, or four-wheeler, and that might push people over the edge.

JOHN BOEVERS: In the wintertime, it's pretty desolate. You get lonely.[1]

CHRIS SCHMIDT: I describe it as a desert tundra. I remember someone visiting from Montana, where there are a lot more trees. He said, "This looks like the Russian tundra. How do people live here?"

KATHLEEN: We all talk about the wintertime blues in Rock Springs. You'll go for nine months without seeing the sun. The wind can be brutal, too. It definitely plays into the drinking because that's something you can do indoors. Unless you're an outdoors person, the climate here can play into addiction very easily.

MIKE: The wind is constant. Even if you get mild temperatures during spring and fall, the wind often cancels it out. You can't think of doing anything outdoors without factoring in the wind.

LISA SPANJERS: The wind blows all the time. And I mean *all the time*. Every weekend I could, I would escape. I had a Camaro and five credit cards, riding high on the hog because I had a good job. But you combine the wind with people drinking constantly and it can get bad. They had to always cancel ball games because the wind was blowing too hard. I couldn't stand the wind. I hated it. Every day I had to work in it. It was depressing. That's why I was always traveling. I couldn't stand to stay in Rock Springs itself for too long.

JIMMY: When I used to ice fish, rabbit hunt, ski, and ride snowmobiles, I didn't mind the winter so much. But I don't do any of that stuff anymore, so the winter is not so great. Next to Rock Springs, I've never seen a community that lives so much for the weekend and vacation during the summer. It's always a ghost town for a couple weeks at the beginning of summer because everyone leaves on vacation, or they go out camping or boating or whatever else.

STACY: When I was a kid, there was a five-hundred-year flood in Rock Springs. We lived pretty close to Bitter Creek, and I remember going to Bunning Park and looking at the floodwaters. That was the first natural devastation I'd seen. There's no escaping nature's brutality when you live there; it has an effect on people. People were struggling already, so it was traumatic for the community to deal with.

The flood was an extreme example, but that brutality was clear all the time. The wind is relentless. It's intense to make it through winter year after year. The first signs of spring take on new meaning. The winters there are their own version of hell. It's cold and constantly windy. Sometimes it snows, which is actually a relief. I remember going to school when it was forty below zero with the wind chill. That nature and terrain end up having a big effect on your being and who you are.

JAY ANSELMI: They say Rock Springs has one of the highest suicide rates in the country. I've always attributed part of it to the wind. I think the wind ends up being the last straw for people. It changes your brain chemistry.

JIMMY: It might not be the main cause, but I really do think the wind plays a role. That fucking wind, dude. I'm a golfer, and I get so pissed sometimes. We don't even say the word "wind" when we're out golfing because we don't want to fucking curse it. It's always something you have to deal with. It's always one more goddamn thing you have to contend with in your life, on top of everything else. It comes at the most inopportune times. It wears on you. People here are strong, but it can get to you.

Sometimes people get mad at the person for checking out. I can understand that in some ways. The one that really fucked me up was my good friend, Benny. I loved that dude. He was in my little crew of friends. He was a sophomore when I was a senior, and he had a heart of gold. I took him hunting. He was such a good person. But I wasn't mad at him when he did it. I personally don't get mad at people when that happens. It's not my personality.

Another good friend of mine died, but it wasn't suicide necessarily. It was an accident. They said he fell off a cliff between Laramie and Fort Collins. He would always go down to Fort Collins to buy pills. I think he pulled off the road to pee and ended up falling off a cliff—but it took him nine hours to die, so he was just suffering there. I think he might've been going down that road anyway before the accident.

It changes you when stuff like that happens. There's a lot of toughness in Rock Springs because there's so much tragedy. One of the coolest things about Rock Springs is, they might talk shit about each other on Facebook all goddamn day, but in the end they really have each other's backs. It reminds me of the Amish in a way, how everyone comes together to raise a barn or help someone in grief. All the different groups come together and make amends for the time being.

DUDLEY GARDNER: There's definitely a community in Rock Springs, but there's not always a lot of emotional support. They say in Rock Springs that you never see your neighbor unless you have a problem, like you need help getting a job done. That's good, but people don't feel so comfortable reaching out for emotional and mental support. We also don't have adequate mental health care and resources in Rock Springs. If people have guns around, they can decide to kill themselves too quickly, before they have a chance to rationalize their problems.

To prevent suicide, you have to reach out to people before they start going down that road so they know they have a community. You can't wait for people to reach that point of desperation. People sometimes have trouble seeing any other choices—and when you have an economy that's so strapped like it is in Wyoming, it's easy to think you don't have any other way out. But of course there are also people who kill themselves who don't fit into any of those patterns. That's really when you can get obsessed with trying to figure out why. People forget that no matter how bad your day is today, tomorrow can be better.

7

Rock Bottom

I grew up in Rock Springs during the nineties, which was the second half of a brutal bust period. I didn't know much about that as a kid, but I do remember a persistent anxiety gnawing at our lives. Money was tight for most people I knew. In one way or another, suicide and addiction seemed to touch everyone in the community. My dad's best friend, an oil field worker, shot himself with a shotgun when I was nine. In junior high, my friends and classmates—many of whom came from families that had been ravaged by drugs and booze—graduated from weed to meth with no middle ground.

Rock Springs was a tough little town in a precarious situation, but people there have always found ways to get by. My dad was an avid hunter and fisherman. Like many families, we rarely ate store-bought meat because we always had deer, elk, antelope, or trout in the freezer. My friends and I rode our BMX bikes in the reaches of dusty prairie surrounding Rock Springs, and local kids started their own punk and metal scene—so in some ways it was as good a place as any to call home. But there was always an underlying uncertainty about what would happen to our town, which bubbled up in destructive ways.

I've heard multiple nicknames for Rock Springs over the years, but Rock Bottom is the one I've encountered most. Each person interviewed here has seen the town's underbelly—and they'll never forget it.

CHELSEA: As far back as I can remember, I didn't want to live in Rock Springs. But I know there are a lot of people who love it there. It's a place where you end up, not a destination to pack up and move to on a whim.

I knew when I lived there that I had to get out for myself. It feels like there aren't options, though. When you grow up there and don't know any different, the high suicide rate is what it is. If you're young and no one has showed you anything else and you're already having a hard time, then you're just like, "Well, fuck. Why even bother?" I certainly had those feelings when I lived there. I'll never be able to say for sure why other people decide to kill themselves, but I think the hopelessness of the place has a lot to do with it. I still feel that hopeless feeling when I go back. I count the days until I get to leave again. I haven't been there for any real amount of time for over eight years.

In Rock Springs, the overall mentality with depression and mental struggles is for people to basically stuff it down and not deal with it—to focus on work and anything else. My mom is very religious, so you were supposed to pray about it or get counseling from your pastor. Generally in the world our approach to mental health is getting better, but in places like Rock Springs the approach is still, "Buck up and deal with your shit on your own time."

I remember drugs and alcohol first being around in seventh grade. I started drinking and smoking pot in eighth grade. Hard drugs were easy to get. I hung out with a lot of older people, too, so that made it even easier. Looking back, it was weird that those older people would want to hang out with kids in junior high. That seemed to happen pretty often in Rock Springs. When I moved, people I knew would never hang out with someone out of high school. I did a lot as a kid. Maybe it's just people who don't leave and get bored and decide to hang out with these younger people. It's weird. Once I was in my early twenties and thought about it, I was like, "I would never hang out with a high school sophomore."

Drugs are for sure an easy trap to fall into there. I've known lots of people who did, myself included for a while. The boredom is part of it. There's nothing else to do, or at least that's what it felt like. I definitely knew people who didn't, but I knew far more who did. And again, I think the hopelessness comes into play. If you don't care and aren't working toward some sort of goal, it's easy to get into drugs because that's what everyone else is doing. I don't want to say you didn't have a choice, because you always do, but it kind of felt like you didn't in a way. Either you're going to go out and party on the weekend, or you're going to sit at home by yourself.

BRIAN: I honestly can't remember a time being happy when I lived in Rock Springs. My parents got divorced when I was five. My mom was doing a lot of drinking and shit, and from that point on I was getting abused. I was only four or five years old the first time I touched a dead body. Neither of my parents were emotionally available. There were just a lot of horrible, horrible things that happened to me.

Overall, it was a very oppressive place. I don't know if it's the weather or just how people are there. It's like this cloud of negativity and depressiveness. It's so blank. I've never been around so many horrible people all at once—and so much intense addiction to alcohol and drugs. It seems like everyone there is trying to block out something.

I was only eight years old the first time I smoked pot and drank. My brother lived under the impression that if he forced me into it, I couldn't tell on him. And then it continued from that point on: he would force me into smoking and drinking with him.

By age eleven I was fully addicted to cigarettes. I used to steal them from Ben's Foodliner. Along with my brother, I started hanging out with some older guys, like Bobby. He was in his thirties, and I was about thirteen. He would buy us alcohol and cigarettes and could get us weed anytime. It was fucked up that he was hanging around thirteen-year-old kids. I would get painkillers and prescription drugs from older people and my friends at school, who'd sometimes trade me cigarettes for pills.

I'm sure you remember how I was in junior high, with the black hair and spikes and all that shit. I was a nice kid, but people were afraid of me. I guess in some cases they had every right to be scared. Being around people in their thirties, I had access to coke, heroin—pretty much anything I wanted. My entire drug addiction was based on the fact that I wanted to die. It wasn't fun for me. There were points when I was selling drugs that it was lucrative and shit like that, but it took me a long time to realize that I was just trying to kill myself without fully pulling the trigger.

TAMMY CURTIS MORLEY: My younger brother is in federal prison for methamphetamine. I found out at my older brother's funeral that he'd tried to kill himself.

MATHIAS: It seems strange to say, but my mental illnesses protected me while I lived in Rock Springs. The self-isolation encouraged by depression and social anxiety kept me from being exposed to the drug scene, more or less. I certainly had friends who used drugs as a coping mechanism. I went to school with peers who were addicted. It still surprises me that I didn't get involved in the drug scene—it's so pervasive.

My mental illnesses were, in part, adaptive coping mechanisms. They cost me immensely and caused me to experience more trauma—and they still do, in some ways—but at the same time, I'm partly grateful for them. I firmly believe that I survived Rock Springs because of the self-imposed isolation, as well as an obsession with being perfect in school and extracurriculars. By nature, I'm an extremely obsessive person, and there are plenty of self-destructive tendencies that live inside me. Had I gotten into the drug scene, I'm not sure that I would've made it out of that town. Perhaps that's naïve and biased of me to think, though.

Now that I can acquire alcohol on my own, whenever I do go back to Rock Springs, I tend to get ridiculously drunk. Drinking is how you survive a desert, after all.

STACY: I definitely saw a lot of alcohol use, and some drug use as well. Teenage drinking wasn't really discouraged. There was a liquor store on Dewar Drive and everyone knew that was the spot where you wouldn't get carded. You'd know to go at a certain time when someone was working. You could just go through the drive-thru. Alcohol is a huge part of Rock Springs culture. There was nothing to do for people but drink and have sex. Part of that seems to be numbing behavior.

GLEN HOOPER: I remember these older dirtbags trying to date girls still in high school and party with them. One of my friends got pregnant from this scummy older guy.

KATHLEEN: When I was younger, I really felt like I didn't fit in here. It felt like everyone drove big trucks and wore camo; and most people are conservative. But that's not everybody here. I think the outsiders are often drawn to each other.

I remember going to punk shows when I was fifteen at the Masonic Temple, train depot, and Knights of Columbus. I felt like I'd found my people. We didn't have much, but the people who got involved were very hands-on. If you go to a city, there are so many options for music and culture. Here, you have to seek it out and create it for yourself.

I was so young when I started going to punk shows. I just knew I didn't want to get involved with the cowboy or jock culture. I'm super grateful I had that experience so I could realize there were other outsiders in town. There were some cool bands, too, like Pennies 4 Porn and Minus the Good Looks. That's how I found out about bands like The Queers. It was a raw scene and might've seemed silly to people from cities—but it's what we had. Everyone had a lot of initiative and a DIY attitude. My friend and I tried to put on a show at the skatepark. It was more work than you might realize.

The local scene seemed to slow down when there was so much underage drinking at the train depot, with kids running around everywhere and puking. I mean, that's the first place I ever drank: one of those shows. It seemed like the mentality was that you needed to get drunk in order to have fun. A lot of those people became alcoholics and partied hard later in life. Lots of people in Rock Springs end up going down that path, probably because there's not much else to do.

PETE: Acid Bath is the Rock Springs soundtrack. A long time ago this crazy tweaker dude with an Acid Bath cassette tape told a bunch of people in town he was the singer, and then the rumor that Dax Riggs lived here started going around. But it was just some random dude.

JOE MYER: I remember everyone in Rock Springs talking about Dax Riggs and Acid Bath, which was so random. I knew about them from growing up around tattoo artists in North Carolina. People in Rock Springs who listened to Hoobastank and shit like that somehow knew Acid Bath. It was cool, just very odd.

JOSH RECKER: There are honestly worse places to live. I made a lot of good friends in Rock Springs and had some great times. We tried to make the local punk scene happen, but it never went anywhere. It's hard when no touring bands stop for shows. Although, with it being right off I-80, pretty much every big band has at least passed through at some point. There's Teenage Bottlerocket from Laramie and the Lillingtons from Newcastle, but there are hardly any other Wyoming bands that are known outside the state.

MATT LEE: You'll never meet anyone in the world like the people you meet from Rock Springs. They're a different breed. They're more hardcore. It's like everything is more intense. It's hard to explain to people who aren't from there. I tell people the stories I have from Rock Springs, and they're always like, "Holy shit, is it really like that there?" It definitely was when I was there. It's just a crazy town, especially since it's right off I-80. It's also a typical small town where everyone is very opinionated and in each other's business. That stuff is really emphasized there. As far as the landscape, it's an arid desert shitshow. I can't stand that shit. It's just a windy-ass desert.

I was actually straight edge until I was about seventeen. I started listening to punk in fourth grade. The kids I hung out with were always older. They were into smoking weed, but we only skated together. I was around drugs and alcohol all the time but was able to separate myself from it. When I was seventeen, my bandmate and I were both depressed because we'd just gotten out of relationships, so we both said, "Fuck it, let's get drunk." We went to the fair and found our friends. They didn't have any alcohol, but they had weed, so that was the first time I ever got high or drunk. It didn't affect me much the first time. The next day I got high as fuck, and then it became a daily thing.

I started drinking not long after that, then I started doing coke in my twenties with my friends who had this crazy party house. Every night, there were at least twenty kids packed in there. It was this little basement apartment. Everyone would hang out and smoke weed and get drunk. Then we all started doing a bunch of coke. After I did coke, I pretty much didn't care anymore. I figured I would try anything. I tried Oxy and felt like I was floating. The next day, my stomach was growling, so I didn't touch it for a while. But then I started dating this girl who liked it, which is when I got hooked.

The boredom and lack of things to do has a lot to do with it. Before I started doing drugs, me and my friends would go to yard sales and buy random cheap shit that we'd take out to the hills to destroy. We'd buy old TVs and record players and smash them with sledge hammers and bats. And we'd light all this shit on fire. The first time I ever did this, I was sixteen and bored as fuck.

Up behind Skyline trailer park is where we'd destroy shit. You could see the interstate from there, so we'd also take golf clubs up there and hit golf balls onto the interstate. I don't think anyone was ever hurt or that we caused any wrecks. We were definitely trying to cause mayhem, though. As I got older, we used to go to the same area and party and still hit golf balls onto the freeway. I've taken my wife up there actually, and we drove some golf balls. You know, keep the tradition alive.

When I started getting fucked up after being straight edge, it felt like I'd finally dropped my guard. Some of my friends from school didn't hang out with me because I didn't drink, so it was a way to connect with people. It was a lot easier to hang out with people if you got high or drunk. The guys in one of my bands were all about hallucinogens like acid, Ecstasy, and mushrooms. That's when I truly started to say, fuck it. There's a lot of peer pressure in Rock Springs, especially for adolescents. It was less, "Do you want to try this?" and more, "It's your fucking turn."

At the same time, I always tried to make the most out of living there with music. But it's tough when it's not encouraged. People like my dad could never see the point if it wasn't making money, and he knew there wasn't much chance of that. A lot of people in Rock Springs have that old school workhorse mentality, where you're either working your ass off or you're failing at life. Being in a band doesn't fit into that worldview; people don't always see the point. It makes it hard to want to keep trying. Either you're working in the oil field or doing manual labor, or there's nothing for you there.

I hate to say this, but I never wanted to end up like my dad. My dad is a great man and awesome person. He works so fucking hard. I just didn't want to base my life on working like that. So many people base their lives off working there. That's all they have and know. It made it so my dad wasn't around much. It also made it so he was an alcoholic. My dad was constantly drinking. I was raised around alcohol, which is why I was straight edge for a long time. So it was either try to stay true to who you are, or just say fuck it and go along with everyone else.

KARA: My dad worked graveyard shifts for a lot of years. I think the sleeping schedule wore him down. He would pretty much drink himself to sleep every day. It was a lifestyle other kids' parents led, too—but nobody really talked about it. It seemed normal, plus there was a lot of shame. You'd listen to Dad's stories and walk on eggshells. Most of his friends who worked at the mine lived the same way. It was definitely more normal than not.

DANELLE: I've come across a lot of parents and people I grew up with who do drugs with their kids. The kids end up thinking it's okay. It blinds them to the bigger realities.

CHRIS SCHMIDT: My dad was the first person I ever saw get high. He thought he was being sneaky and didn't realize I was watching him when he was getting high in the shed. I was in seventh or eighth grade. The first time I ever smoked weed, it was my dad's weed, which he'd just barely hidden in the garage. It took me two seconds to find. Since my dad was the first person I saw use drugs, I didn't have the stigma that some kids are brought up with surrounding drugs. I wasn't inundated with the idea that drugs are negative, like a lot of people are. My dad was somewhat successful in the community, so I didn't think it was a big deal. That was the mentality I had going into it.

My friends and I started getting high in the desert area that stretched behind our school. We would go into the little ravines and ditches and smoke weed, ride bikes, and just be dumb kids. There's so much space out there, where no one is out checking on you. This was before there were any houses in that area.

Maybe it was because our junior high was on the newer side of town, I'm not sure, but it was always presented to me that kids at East Junior High were doing drugs since sixth grade. People at my school didn't get into it until a bit later. When I met kids from East, they were way gnarlier than any of us. I ended up getting along with you guys a lot better than most people at my school. In Rock Springs, drugs are a way of life for a lot of people—and a way to deal with living there. So many drugs flow through the town on I-80. It only makes sense that a lot of people would have drug problems.

Like I said, using drugs felt natural for me. My dad and all his friends got high. There wasn't much guidance as far as experimenting responsibly or in a reasonable fashion. Rock Springs during the seventies was fucking nuts, so I don't think my dad really knew how to address it with me, which is why my parents ended up sending me away. I had a solid group of friends outside partying, and we didn't drink together until later—but with everyone else, doing cocaine and pills and eventually meth really felt like I was going with the flow. It all seemed very normal.

I remember my girlfriend at the time telling me she couldn't hang out because she'd gotten grounded. When I asked her how she got in trouble, she said her mom found a lightbulb under her bed. I didn't understand and had to look it up on the internet. I remember thinking, "What the fuck? You're smoking *meth*?" We were in junior high. Seeing people around me using drugs from such a young age really took away the taboo element of it that other kids might've had.

I started to realize that the things people had been saying about meth being everywhere were true. Once I started actually looking for it and being able to spot it at parties and stores—once I understood what that lifestyle looks like—I remember thinking, "Oh shit, meth really is everywhere here."

DAN SHINEBERG: My mom started working for CPS at one point. Meth-related cases completely overshadowed everything else. Her coworkers didn't know what to do.

NATE MARTIN: From what I saw, it was so clear that meth was a bad idea. Everyone I knew that did it had severe problems—and they just looked fucked up. To this day, I've never tried it, even though it was the most omnipresent of the hard drugs of my youth.

Around the time my friends and I first started becoming cognizant of drug culture, I remember my friend asking, "Why do people here always say 'smoking crack' when everybody does crank?" I remember that to this day: everybody does crank. Everyone has bonkers stories about meth. My friend's mom was addicted to it. I remember him telling me that he always knew when she'd relapsed because he'd wake up and the house would be perfectly clean. She'd stay up all night scrubbing the house.

When my other friend was staying in the trailer court by Walmart, he and my buddy found a Crown Royal bag full of meth. It was like thirty thousand dollars' worth of meth. There was also a little speaker magnet in there. The bag was right near this speed bump. They were only around sixteen years old. They figured someone had this big bag underneath their car, using the speaker magnet to hold it in place. When they hit the speed bump, they hit it a little too fast and shook the bag off. But my buddies didn't want to fuck with meth. They also didn't know what to do with it.

So they ended up selling it to my friend's mom for like $300. I'm not sure what she did with it, but that's the type of thing someone could get killed over: thirty thousand dollars' worth of drugs.

JOE MYER: I ended up getting stuck in Rock Springs on my twenty-first birthday. I was at this house where they were passing around Jäger bottles . . . and then I woke up in jail. They charged me with nine felony crimes. I was like, "Wait, but what did I do?" Really I was just outside at the wrong place at the wrong time. They somehow decided I was the person who'd been breaking into all the charter buses for the oil field guys. I was so confused. A day before I was in San Diego. I really was.

The cops finally did what they call a presentencing investigation and said, "We've tracked down that you were in San Diego the day before you were arrested because we found a receipt in your evidence." I'd been telling them exactly that for the past fourteen days. They said they had to do their due diligence, but really they wanted to fuck with me, the twenty-one-year-old from out of state who had no ID. They still stuck me with drinking underage—because I was technically twenty when I was arrested—being drunk in public, and resisting arrest. They gave me six months' probation and these huge fines.

In my head I was like, "Okay, I'll stay and work and pay it off and then leave." I got a job at the Taco John's next to Ace Hardware. I couldn't make fuck-all for money. They paid me six dollars an hour and made me the manager because I was the oldest person there.

We'd only stopped in Rock Springs during our road trip so my buddy could get money from his mom, who worked at the Jim Bridger power plant. He said that on our way to Miami, we were going to stop at his mom's, and he told me all his friends were cool and were going to show me a great time for my birthday. Six months later I was strung out in Rock Springs and asking my dad in North Carolina if I could come home and sleep on his floor. I'm from the East Coast and didn't know about meth yet. When I tried it, I remember thinking, "Where's this been all my life?" I had a few bad months on that bullshit.

CHRIS HAWKS: My wife's dad was a pharmacist at City Market, and during the bust of the nineties, he was robbed. He got destroyed during that recession. He was down from this huge store to just one pharmacy counter. He was about sixty-seven or sixty-eight and was barely scraping by. Smith's stores had moved into communities and crushed the local businesses. He was robbed at gunpoint in the pharmacy by an opioid addict. The guy came in with a gun, cleaned out the cash, cleaned out the drugs, and left. It was scary shit.

MARY: There's nothing to do but get fucked up on drugs. And there are always so many rumors going around about people. One of my friends gave his girlfriend morphine without knowing she was allergic to it. She died while they were fucking. He ended up going to prison. People are so quick to give up on you. They started saying he was trying to kill her on purpose.

DAN SHINEBERG: My family helped keep me away from the darker side of Rock Springs. My mother was a probation officer. She was one of the first four women probation officers in Wyoming—and the only female probation officer on the west side of the state. When you're nine or ten and you hear that you'll spend a night in jail if you try drugs, it sends a strong message. She was honest and straightforward about it. She said, "If I see it or find out about it, I'll call the police, and you and your brother can spend the night in jail. You can go talk to Judge Souleil or Judge James, and I know you go to school with James's daughter." She left it up to us: do you want to have a bad experience, or do you just not want to go there? My father died when we were in school. Same with my grandma. We didn't want to disappoint her. I never went there in high school.

My grandparents knew everyone in the community, and if that's the case, you don't want to step out of line because it will be an embarrassment. You also have a lot of expectations from adults in school. The worst thing I ever did was get a Ouija board and some candles with my friend who was interested in whatever Wiccan crap, and we went to a cemetery to play Ouija on Halloween night.

A cop followed us out there. He turned on his light as soon as we started. He knew exactly who I was and said, "Mr. Shineberg?" He was my mom's friend, so I called him by his first name. He said, "No, it's *Officer* Christiansen." I was just like, "Oh, crap." He searched all our stuff and couldn't find any drugs, so he said, "Were you guys seriously just out here playing Ouija?" He couldn't wait to tell his cop friends. It became a big joke at the police department. I got grounded for it. As stupid as it was, that experience reinforced that I couldn't get away with anything without it getting out.

You always knew which kids were using. You could tell by the scab marks and sheen their skin took on. It was obvious, and they weren't getting help.

CHELSEA: I wonder all the time if I would be here if I hadn't left Rock Springs. I really broke down when I was there. I begged my parents to let me leave. I was definitely spiraling in the months before I left and remember thinking I was either going to die or get arrested. I had gotten lucky so many times, and I knew it wasn't going to last forever.

GLEN HOOPER: I started drinking heavily and smoking pot around eighth and ninth grade. I know a lot of people want to pretend like everything is okay in Rock Springs, but there's a lot going on beneath the surface. I got thrown in jail for weed a few times. That's what they do there: lock you up without trying to solve the problem.

I started hanging out with some older kids who knew a bunch of people around town. They'd let these drifters stay with them, which happened a lot since Rock Springs is right on the interstate. It's so easy for people to bring drugs in. This one guy had acid and meth. That's when I started tripping on LSD and pretty much doing any drug that came my way. Except meth. I was huffing carburetor cleaner at my job, but for some reason I drew the line at meth. My friend and I ended up having a bad mushroom trip in California. We hitch-hiked back to Wyoming, barefoot. My mom was working all the time, so the only one around was my grandma, who was pretty much deaf and blind. So yeah, it wasn't hard to get away with stuff.

Drugs were always around. A lot of kids' parents were getting high and partying, too. There was both a meth epidemic *and* an opioid epidemic in Rock Springs, and I'm pretty sure it's the same now. There are very few options and resources for youth there. You'd see the football players and all kinds of people at parties where you knew exactly what was happening, like everyone was doing coke or whatever else.

A lot of people want to make some quick cash, especially when it's during a bust in the town. I've known a lot of people who try to sell a little here and there and end up paying the price, whether it's in jail or their own lives. There was an entire family out in Superior that got busted for running a meth ring. It was something like twenty of them.

My friend and I sold a little weed, except I was never good at it, because I just smoked it all. I lived with this older guy, and my friend ended up owing him some money. The guy pulled a knife on him even though it was only a couple hundred bucks' worth of weed.

At one point, I had a vial of LSD and spilled a bunch of it on my tongue—a lot more than I'd meant to. It must've been at least twenty hits, but who knows. I tripped for eight days straight. I got thrown in jail. They thought I was insane because they didn't know anything about drugs. I wasn't eating right and was just extremely fucked up by the end of it. That's when my mom put me in rehab.

For whatever reason, my mom was sure she didn't want to put me in Southwest Counseling. No one ever had anything positive to say about that place. She's actually been sober for thirty-two years and goes to AA all the time. But I only made better drug connections in rehab. It's true what they say about how jail and a lot of those places mostly teach you how to be a better criminal.

The doctors didn't give a shit about teaching people how to be sober and actually helping us. A lot of them were straight-up assholes. They diagnosed me with schizophrenia because of the tripping. They were completely off. They threw me on antipsychotic meds that made me feel nothing. I was a zombie, just totally gray. There was nothing in there about teaching us about sober living or finding other outlets after rehab, except maybe a shitty video they made us watch.

I honestly can't believe I survived some of that shit. I don't know why I was driving this one night, because I couldn't even walk, let alone drive. I was with my two friends, and we ended up spinning out at the bottom of this big hill. That type of stuff happens all the time there. If it's not suicide, people die in car wrecks from driving drunk and doing other crazy shit. An old friend of mine who wasn't even forty just died. They said it was a heart attack, but who knows in Rock Springs. That happens a lot when people OD or kill themselves: they don't say it in the obituaries.

My other friend tried to kill himself in fourth grade. He slit his wrists but survived because he did it the wrong way. The first time someone I knew died by suicide was this girl I was friends with, Shoshanna. I remember her being very kind to people. She had a bad acid trip and no one helped her. She broke into a gun store and shot herself. That popular guy in high school was another. One kid jumped off this huge cliff at a party at Flaming Gorge; they never found his body. Two other kids OD'd on pain pills a few years after high school. Whenever I scroll through Facebook, it seems like I find out about another death there.

No one ever really talked to us about suicide. It was the Rock Springs thing of trying to sweep it all under the rug and pretend like everything is okay. I remember one stupid video in health class after a kid shot himself. I don't even know if we had a school counselor.

I dropped out of school when I was eighteen. I called my sister, who was living in Houston, and told her I was going to die if I stayed in Rock Springs. I could see that's how it was going to end for me there. I moved down to Texas and started work as a machinist, which I've done since then. In Houston, no one knew me. There was no one who knew my past and could say that's who I was going to be for the rest of my life. My sister and I lived in the Third Ward. I just stuck to myself. I was able to focus a lot on playing music. It was good because it taught me how to fend for myself.

NATE MARTIN: I didn't really think about the suicide rate being so high until I left, although I did go to school with a girl who killed herself. She was really cool. She played bass. She ended up shooting herself in the head with a shotgun a few years after she and I lost touch. She lived in an apartment underneath the gun store and killed herself inside the store.

BRIAN: One of the things that really made me feel lost was when my friend, Shoshanna, killed herself. She was about five years older than me. I vividly remember hanging out with her for the first time. My brother was dating this girl named Amber, and we were hanging out at my mom's house. At one point my brother and his girlfriend went into the other room, which was just behind this curtain. We could clearly hear them fucking. I was just hanging out and smoking weed and drinking with Shoshanna.

About a week later, she did a lot of acid and freaked out. She ended up breaking into a gun store. They say she shot herself, but I believe the cops shot her. I was crying in school the next day and ended up getting illegally detained and taken down to the police station because they thought I was going to shoot up the school. Someone had decided to say that for no reason, other than they thought I was weird and scary. The cops searched me. There was a gun at home, but it wasn't on me. After that, my parents wouldn't let me go to a normal school.

J.J. ANSELMI: There was this kid I went to junior high with who shot himself playing Russian Roulette with his buddies. Not long before that, a substitute teacher I'd had a few times killed himself by running his car with the garage door closed. I remember people not being surprised, like it was just a regular thing.

PETE: The first suicide I dealt with was Deshawn. I've known five people who killed themselves, plus all the others who've overdosed. It always feels so close to home.

MARY: I honestly think the way people constantly talk behind your back there contributes to the suicide rate. It's such a small town. Everything gets around so quick, but it's never really the truth. There might be one thing about the rumor that's true, but it's almost never the whole story that's true. People constantly make shit up and add it to whatever rumor is going around. It can create a lot of depression and pressure from getting talked about all the time, like you have no control. After a while, it can make people want to give up. It makes you lose faith in people and feel like you're not safe anywhere. It makes you feel unwelcome in the place where you grew up.

One of my best friends, Deshawn, killed herself when I was fifteen. That was the first suicide in my life, and it hit me extremely hard. James was at our house right before he killed himself. Same with Greg, although we never knew for sure if his overdose was on purpose. I do think it was suicide with pills, though.

James's death fucked up a lot of people. He was the hot guy in school. Everybody loved him. We never knew what could've possibly been so bad that he couldn't tell anybody—that made him feel like we wouldn't love him anymore. Nobody knew what could've been so bad. He couldn't have done anything that bad, to the point where that was the route to take. He couldn't have done anything to make people hate him, because he was such a good person. It breaks your heart to think that people get to a place where they feel like there's no other way out.

I don't remember anyone talking to us at school about suicide. Just drugs. I don't remember bullying or suicide being a big issue as far as teachers and staff talking to students. Adults didn't talk to us like those things were big problems in our community. There was nothing about how to prevent suicide, or how to see the tell-tale signs. We weren't taught those things, like it wasn't a big enough issue for that to happen. They taught us about drugs and signs to watch out for if your friend's addicted—never much about bullying or suicide, though.

There were a lot of times when Rock Springs felt like one big family. Everyone was friends with everyone else. My brother was a popular football player. He made it a point to invite everyone to parties and include everyone. As far as people not talking about suicide, I don't think people want to admit that it happens so close to home. No one wants to admit their family isn't perfect, that they don't have the perfect kids and life. They don't want to open their eyes to that reality.

ANDREA: Looking at why the suicide rate is high can be tough because it can differ so much between people in terms of why they do it. The suicide that had the most impact on me was one of my students. He was so smart and well liked. It seemed like that kid had everything going for him. Except for something. So the question of why is always there, and I don't know if you ever find the full answer. He was so young. It was very hard to be a teacher at that time and realize one of your students was hurting like that.

I've heard lots of reasons. I've heard people say it's the wind, or it's the alcohol, or it's that feeling that things will never get better, that despair. I've talked with people who say they've gotten in the car and just had these urges to drive off the road. Ultimately, I don't know. There are so many possible reasons. Some people do it for health reasons, if they're sick and don't want to go on anymore. The isolation and the weather might also be connected to the despair. You see people and they seem so happy and like they're really getting along—and then boom, they're gone.

DAN SHINEBERG: I remember being at school the day after James killed himself. It was like an explosion had gone off. His grandma was the school secretary. She fought through her grief like no one I'd ever seen before.

J.J. ANSELMI: James's suicide was heavy for our entire high school. Afterward, I remember sitting through one health class about suicide and trying to prevent it—but when it's such a pervasive problem in your community, you need to address it with kids earlier on and much more often. They need to know you don't have to be ashamed of those feelings, how to reach out to someone, and who they can talk to.

DAN SHINEBERG: There seemed to be a lot of apathy about suicide in our generation. People would joke about it because they didn't understand it. I remember a few students trying to create an awareness of self-harm, and they had some teacher support. Those students had personal experience with self-harm and suicidal ideation. But the principal shut them down. He thought talking about it would only give people ideas, and then they'd want to do it themselves. After that, one of those students cut herself. The principal and guidance counselor said that was exactly why they didn't want people to talk about it. They thought that, if you didn't talk about it, it would go away. That's how mental health was treated.

STACY: I don't think there was much of an approach to mental health or access to resources at all. It just didn't exist. It wasn't something we ever thought about, which is wild to look back on. No real crisis services at all. I definitely knew people who weren't in the best mental state while there. Mental health wasn't something we were educated on as youth, even as far as identifying when someone might be in a bad spot and you might need to intervene.

MIKE: There have been multiple acquaintances of mine who've killed themselves or overdosed. I haven't been personally connected to anyone who died by suicide, although my grandfather killed himself before I was born. So it's something that's impacted my family in a big way. He was a Korean war veteran and killed himself in the early sixties. It had a huge impact on my mom, especially as she was dealing with being bipolar.

My mom dealt with a lot of mental health concerns in her life. I don't think she ever got the care she needed. Part of that was definitely because she lived in Wyoming. There's a lot of stigma attached to mental illness there. She's dealt with a lot of ups and downs and bipolar-type issues. But she never wanted to take medication because of the bad experiences she had with the Wyoming mental health infrastructure. She was against therapy and pharmacological help for the majority of her life. She dealt with it all on her own.

DAN SHINEBERG: When you live in a hard-working, weathered community that has a history of trauma, you need to acknowledge it and try to make a change.

8

Home of 56 Nationalities

When you take the first Rock Springs exit from I-80 East, you see a massive American flag on a towering white pole.[1] In front of the pole, there's a stone sign with "Rock Springs / Home of 56 Nationalities" etched into it. Seeing as how most of those nationalities are European, it's a misleading slogan, much like the myth that America is a melting pot.

What the sign doesn't say is that Rock Springs is overwhelmingly white—or that, like much of the rural West, it's a bastion of heteronormativity and rigid masculinity. Growing up, I never asked any of the marginalized people I knew what it was like to live in such a place. It wasn't until 2020, when I interviewed people over the phone from 850 miles away, that I finally did.[2]

DANELLE: It's very small. They have the catchphrase that it's "Home of 56 Nationalities," but it's mostly white people.

CHRIS SCHMIDT: Rock Springs historically has some diversity, but when I lived there, it was not a diverse place. People came from across the country for the oil boom. That's about it.

BRIAN: When I worked in an oil field shop in Riverton, the racism toward Native people was pretty staggering, even though we were technically living on their land. They've been there for literally thousands of years. Racism is just very prevalent in Wyoming. You'd be disgusted by the stuff you'd hear coming out of people's mouths. It's very common and accepted. You hear otherwise decent people say horrible things.

WING LEW: My ex-wife told me about some kids mocking her and pretending to speak Chinese down at the mechanic's shop.

MATHIAS: The xenophobia and racism that led to the deaths of twenty-eight Chinese miners is in that land today. I know the general area where the Rock Springs Massacre happened, where Chinatown was razed by fire. I drive by it and have visited the memorial with their names, just to remember. I remember, knowing that the violence done to the land through mining has also led us toward the climate crisis as much as it's destroyed the human bodies that have done that labor.

Rock Springs's threads of xenophobia and racism have deeply impacted who I am. I've had to unlearn so much. The town has a lot of transient labor shifting in and out with the mines, with oil and gas. There's a deep distrust of outsiders in a town where old families have a lot of power, and where I had no access to queer mentors or role models. It's a town that people often leave and never come back—but also a town that many are afraid they'll never be able to leave in the first place.

MIKE: If I remember correctly, it's 88 or 89 percent white. I may be a bit off on that, but it's in the ballpark. I have a friend who likes to brag about how Wyoming has no racism.

There was such a whitewashing of Wyoming history for us throughout school. We didn't hear much at all about the Chinese Massacre. I didn't learn about the Black Fourteen until much later. They were fourteen African American football players at the University of Wyoming that all got kicked off the team in 1969 for wearing black armbands in solidarity with the anti-racism movement. We never heard anything about that in school.

ORLANDO WEBB: Yeah, I've experienced racism here. No matter where you go, even in a small place like this, it's going to be there. It might not be seen or out in the open as much, and people might not pay attention unless it's happening to them. In high school it happened. We had one bad year where it was happening all the time. But as people grow up, they see the error of their ways and they change—at least you hope they do. Racism is everywhere you go, even though you might not always see it. People in communities like this might try to sweep it under the rug, but a rug can only cover up so much dirt.

During my senior year, we had people calling our house on weekends and saying some really horrendous things. Someone told one of my cousins they were going to hang him from a building. Our pastor had to come to school to intervene. It was a week-in, week-out thing to deal with—with people making those calls on the weekends, or saying things at school but then denying it to your face. When confronted, none of those people had anything to say. We knew who they were.

No one put a stop to it, really, so it got out of control. People graduated and moved away, and that's just what it is. Sometimes when you stand up to a bully, it works. Other times it doesn't. That hatred is learned and connects to how people are raised. They see it, they learn it, and no one ever tells them different. They don't know any better, and it becomes part of their personality.

It's something I've learned to deal with, because you know it's going to happen. Of course you want the world to change and people to learn, and of course we've come a long way since the beginning of our country. But there's still a long way to go. I try not to let it affect my life because it's always going to be there. Someone's always going to say something about your race, gender, or wherever you come from. If you let that break you down every time, you're never going to move past it. I try to rise above it, but it can be harder to do by yourself than people realize.

DANELLE: We were taught that we could either ignore racism or stand up for ourselves. We stood up for ourselves. There were a lot of us growing up at the same age, so it was easier to stand up for ourselves as a group rather than getting singled out.

There was a lot of stereotyping. People were taught that instead of actually knowing what they're talking about. There was name-calling and people telling us we'd end up in prison. People would also try to exclude us—but because we were athletes, we were more up in the popular crowd than some of those kids, who we didn't associate ourselves with.

That's what a lot of people here have been taught. It's what they've grown up with in their households. Young kids get into it because it's what their parents believe. They find people on the same path and end up running with each other.

Trump getting elected definitely made people feel like they had permission to be louder about their racism. It seems more common now than when I was growing up. People think it's okay because of him. I see a lot of Confederate flags around town.

They actually had a Trump rally outside the high school. It felt dangerous. They didn't seem fully educated on what they were standing for, and it felt like they were against people of color and anyone who didn't like Trump. It was scary.

ALICIA: Being a mixed kid, I never felt like I fit in. I had friends, you know—I played with the neighborhood kids and my cousins. I grew up in an area of Rock Springs that we called Motown because all four blocks were Black families. I grew up in the house my mother grew up in. When my grandpa died, he left them the house.

It could be difficult with the other Black girls. I was bullied by some of them until I was sixteen, but I stood up to them during sophomore year. They didn't like me because I'm pretty and have lighter skin. As we got older, that became very evident. When we were in sixth grade, one of those girls got the entire class to stop talking to me. So there was a lot of not feeling like I fit in, feeling like an outcast. Plus I was an only child. My mother fostered in me, at a very young age, a love for reading and learning. When I went into seventh grade, I had a college reading level. So I found connections in books.

I experienced racism from both sides. While some of the Black kids were calling me derogatory names, I was experiencing racism from white students as well. I'll never forget one AP biology class when a white girl looked at me and said, "I guess they'll let just anybody into this class." You learned to develop a really thick skin early on.

When I was in junior high, we were the first class to use those state proficiencies that came out. My science teacher kept failing me and having me redo projects. We had to build a model of a house and have it wired so the lights worked. My dad and I worked hard on that house, and it turned out amazingly. It had furniture, a staircase, wiring, everything. It was an actual doll house. She gave me a C while giving white students who turned in half-assed cardboard houses As. The Rock Springs library later requested to put my house on display. All the teacher ever said was that it wasn't done correctly. That was the feedback.

In high school, I also dealt with racism from a few teachers. Our Spanish teacher's daughter married a Black man, and the teacher was not happy about it. I was the only Black person in class. He said, "Alicia, when you see the picture, you'll know why I'm upset." He showed the picture to the entire class. He ended up getting into some professional trouble because of that.

That science teacher from junior high started teaching at the high school when I was there. Thankfully, I had a different science teacher then. He gave me high marks on all my proficiencies. One day I saw the other science teacher in the hall, and she said, "Well, if it isn't the proficiency queen." So yeah, racism was all around me. It was always there.

You could feel racial tension from the minute you walked into a room. Being the only Black girl on the dance and cheerleading teams, I can tell you that half the girls didn't care for people of color. And I can tell you their parents had the same hatred. It's sad that we still live in a society where that could be the case.

Some of the teachers were afraid to go against the parents and speak out against racism taught in the home. For one, there's a lot of old money in Wyoming. You have a lot of old families and old ties. To go against the grain wasn't something many teachers wanted to do. They knew the parents would go to the school board.

When I went to a dance with a white guy, it was high school news. I know he got a lot of shit from his peers for that. In junior year, a group of white students yelled out to my boyfriend when I was with him, calling him an n-word lover. This was in 2004. So while they say it's the Home of 56 Nationalities, it's not inclusive. I've talked to Asian and Latinx people who moved into town and said they were ostracized as well.

I've had to check several people for making racist comments over the years. They'll say, "Well, I don't mean anything by it," so I let them know about the historical context and that it's not acceptable. They're uneducated when it comes to the world and how oppression gets reinforced.

MIKE: There were a handful of teachers at our high school that, in retrospect, did an amazing job and brought some crucial perspectives into the classroom. Mrs. Jasper was a radical African American feminist teacher, and she was such a force in that school. She impacted so many people's lives and really took on the challenge of teaching in a place like that.

J.J. ANSELMI: It's hard to truly fathom what an important teacher Gigi Jasper was for Rock Springs High School. Those kids and their parents who've spoken out against her have no comprehension of how vital her teaching was, and how hard she worked to give students a picture of what the world is really like. I know she faced some very intense pushback when she tried to teach kids about police brutality and profiling, like parents writing furious letters to the editor of the local newspaper. She also faced in-person hostility from racist students. You have to think about how driven and strong a person would have to be to continue on in an environment like that—and how much you'd have to genuinely care about those kids. Some of the stories of what students have said, and how they've threatened her, are completely vile.

When I had Mrs. Jasper in school, she finished her PhD at NYU. I remember her mentioning it sort of off-handedly, like it wasn't this huge accomplishment.

WES CARTER: I will say that I've been racially profiled a lot here. There are only a few Black people in town. Most of the profiling has been from the Rock Springs police. I was also racially profiled when I worked in the oil field. I walked off one job because of it.

There's racism here for sure, but it's not the most racist place I've ever lived. It was really bad in Tennessee. That said, I remember being aware at a young age that Rock Springs is mostly white people.

I was on a bike ride with my son, and a cop pulled up next to us and said I had to go with him. I asked if I could at least take my son home. I ended up spending three months in jail. The local newspaper said I endangered my children. That's not me. They slandered my name. The charges were dismissed, but I'll never get that time in my life back. You can make money again, but you can't get the time back. My kids have never been in danger. There's been other times when the cops stopped me and asked me questions for no reason. I could fill an entire book if I went all the way back.

I'm still glad I was raised here. My family raised me right.

BRIAN: There is this very real undertone of racism, homophobia, and bigotry in Wyoming. No one wants to be upfront and say it, but it's there. I've known lots of people that didn't come out until they left. I've known a few trans people who said they never would've embraced themselves in Rock Springs, because it isn't accepted, or even safe. But now they're comfortable enough where they live to be themselves.

MATHIAS: There honestly is a lot I don't remember from my childhood and teenage years. My memory has been impaired somewhat by trauma. I also completely disconnected from everything and everyone as soon as I got to junior high. It wasn't a safe place for me. Part of the disconnection was influenced by an eating disorder that was at its worst when I was about thirteen. That eating disorder was in and of itself due to gender norms that led me to think my only worth as someone assigned female at birth was thinness. It's taken a long time for me to unpack, but what I really longed for then was androgyny. I didn't know how to get there, or even what I was really after. The gender norms were rigidly binary. I was never around anyone that defied them, except perhaps those who would call themselves tomboys. Androgyny didn't really exist, at least not when I was in Rock Springs.

Because of the eating disorder and my depression, I came to

refuse to wear makeup or dress in anything other than sweatpants and T-shirts. Dress clothes were always uncomfortably tight for me. I never felt like I could breathe in them. In retrospect, that was because dress clothes are ridiculously gendered. I never dared to think I could wear anything that wasn't from the women's aisles in stores. So I avoided gender norms in how I dressed, whenever I could.

I remember when a friend asked me to prom. I didn't realize it wasn't going to be just the two of us going. She had a date; I was asked along as a friend. I thought I had to wear a dress. My mom even said that if I wore pants, people would think I was a lesbian. I hate dresses. So I borrowed my sister's dress. And then I went and realized it wasn't only the two of us. I didn't know how to dance in heels, so after thirty minutes I came home alone, crying in my car. That was the only school dance I ever went to.

The homophobia in Rock Springs was extreme enough that I assumed I was simply asexual when I had no interest in dating men. It never crossed my mind I could be lesbian. And it certainly never crossed my mind that maybe I myself wasn't a woman. While I'm still on the asexual spectrum, the problem was that I never thought other aspects of queerness were an option for me. I knew only one openly gay student, although since graduating high school, my friend group realized that we're almost all queer. It's really only queer folk that I keep in contact with now from my high school days.

My first real understanding of marginalization and a sense of having to pass as normal—read: mentally healthy, cisgender, straight—came from living with depression and anxiety. I knew since I was in about fifth grade that I could never be myself. The knowledge simply evolved from there as I grew older. Teenagers by nature are rebellious and challenge authority, which explains some of my angst. But looking back there was absolutely an additional layer of distance. There was absolutely more than one reason as to why I felt like and embraced a notion of being an outsider.

Sometimes I think about what might have been and how much better of an experience I would've had if I simply had access to more queer adults. More queer mentors. More openly queer students. Had I known that gender is a construct, that it's not binary. Had I been able to admit to myself that yes, I had crushes on my friends. Had I not used an obsession with band and music to be the only thing that I was, because it was a safer identity than queerness. Had I let my attraction to women be something I could celebrate rather than something I weaponized against myself to further self-hatred and my ongoing relationship with eating disorders. I sometimes cannot believe this was my experience in 2010.

I still don't feel like I can be myself when I go back to Rock Springs. Existing as a nonbinary, genderqueer person in any space means that I often can't pass as either straight or cisgender. There are certainly places and people that I avoid whenever I'm back. I have more guardedness with me when in my hometown. I'm not a fan of using the term "coming out"—I think it's a lot more complicated than many realize and is often used as a stereotype for the queer community—but I never really "came out" in that town.

I've come back as an openly queer person, and I've essentially told some people individually; but otherwise, whenever I return to Rock Springs, I find little reason to authentically engage with people. I've also never really brought a partner home. I don't know how I would navigate the town with someone I love. Sometimes I think about what a high school reunion would look and feel like for me—and then I remember that literally no one knew who I was, that I can't really go back. Nor do I want to.

One thing that still haunts me: since living as openly queer, I've never gone back to the Bike & Trike. That bike shop meant everything to me in my teenage years. Their weekly shop rides taught me about technical skills in terms of how to ride a bike. They also helped me a lot with social anxiety and learning how to be okay just being with fellow humans. Growing up, the bike shop was a space where I could be myself. There were no expectations of me other than to have fun mountain biking with some really rad people.

I know folks at the shop would be supportive and affirming of my queerness now. But the shop was so important to me during my last few years in Rock Springs that it still feels like too much to risk losing. So I haven't been back.

MIKE: For a lot of years, I definitely had an aversion to talking about Rock Springs. I wanted to disconnect. I haven't spent more than three or four consecutive days there since 2005. In three or four years, I will have spent as much time outside Wyoming as I did living there.

I've had to do a lot of unlearning as far as what I internalized there. You have the cowboy archetype that influences everything. The state really leans into that as a whole—and not only with the mascot, but with the outlook and attitude. There's a lot of machismo and rigidity when it comes to gender and sexuality. You don't get much variation.

Throughout my childhood and growing up, I was constantly trying to explore myself and the things I was interested in. But I'd always hit a wall, almost immediately. I would get called out if I stepped outside the norm. While I didn't get bullied a whole lot, I do remember there being a constant vigilance for anything that stepped outside that typical masculine presentation and identity. I used to love playing with my sister's toys. I loved Britney Spears and Christina Aguilera and the freedom they seemed to have to express their femininity. But there was always the question of why: *Why do you like that type of music?* Older men in my family and my peers really looked down on that type of thing. I was a huge Britney fan since around '98 or '99. I remember having to disguise my fandom as an attraction to her. The culture is so stifling that you can't even develop your own interests before you run into some sort of wall.

As a not-your-typical masculine boy, I learned early on to have a public-facing persona that wasn't who I actually was, although I'm not sure how well I performed being a typical boy. I must not have done too well. I thought I was doing a good job, though. I felt like I could like what I liked, but I just had to hide it.

I didn't have many male friends because I felt like girls didn't scrutinize me in the same way. I've never understood that rigidity, where we have to look at even the types of music people like to see if it's masculine or feminine enough. There's a lot of misogyny in that as well: you couldn't like a female artist beyond thinking she's hot. In high school, I started gravitating toward queer voices, even though I wouldn't allow myself to identify that way. Things were bubbling below the surface, but it didn't seem like an option to explore that.

I was in seventh or eighth grade when Matthew Shepard was murdered in Laramie. That was psychologically earth-shattering to me. I remember being frozen as some of the teachers talked about it. There was a numbness. It was frightening in a very primal way. But again, I wouldn't let myself delve into those feelings.

There were some discussions at school. Teachers obviously thought it was tragic, but it didn't lead to any reckoning with homophobia or call for meaningful change. You had people doing backflips to avoid the reality that it was a hate crime. They wouldn't call it what it was. There was a lot of character assassination, with people attributing the murder to Shepard being on drugs and getting himself into a bad situation. There was a lot of defensiveness that, looking back, reminds me of white fragility, with people not willing to see racism because of the guilt they might feel. It seemed like people dismissed him as being a drug addict so they wouldn't have to get into the underlying reality of homophobia.

I think in the state as a whole there was this refusal to reckon with its homophobia after Matthew Shepard. I don't think it's the same situation it was back in 1999, as there are some gay pride events in Casper and Cheyenne, but I think Rock Springs in particular still lacks support for queer identities. There's no celebration of queerness, just rage against people who don't check off all the boxes of heteronormativity.

I've run into the idea of tolerance there a lot. People saying stuff like, "I'm fine with gay people, but I just don't want it shoved in my face." If you amend your statement with a "but," it's antiqueer. People think they're being moderate when they say that. In reality, you're effectively saying you don't want queerness around, which is hateful. For almost two decades, that type of hate and heteronormativity was shoved down my throat. There was also a lot of the stereotype that gay people should be pitied, as if you could never find happiness.

So for me, getting out of Wyoming was essential. It wasn't a choice. Even when I wasn't aware of who I was, I was aware I didn't belong there. There are still times when I feel the need to perform straightness where I am, but I'm much more able to be myself.

There were rumors about a few queer teachers in Rock Springs. They weren't able to be who they were in public. So the only version of gay adulthood I remember seeing was that it's fodder for rumors and nasty gossip. I'm out with my students now. While that discussion is a challenge every year, knowing an openly queer adult when I was a kid would've been so powerful to me. I want kids to know there's a future for them. I work with queer students now and try to teach them about coping skills and ways to celebrate queerness.

JACK WATERS: You know as well as I do that it takes tough motherfuckers to grow up here. Now imagine growing up in Rock Springs being gay. Now imagine working as a nurse at the hospital for thirty years as an openly gay man. If someone can't deal with it, I just say, "Whelp, see you later, dude. I was without you before you talked to me, and I'll be without you after you quit talking to me."

I grew up as a "sissy." My brother was an athlete. My dad's dad died when he was in seventh grade. All my dad knew was sports. He almost got a taste of my grandma's skillet when I was in eighth grade because he called me a sissy. Well, that sissy put himself through college in Wyoming and went on to thrive in the community as a health-care professional.

Growing up here was eased by having all my family here. My dad's family was original Superior, back when the mine out there was still running. All my cousins lived here. We all grew up together. Our grandparents grew up in this house, so we all had a very special bond. My brothers and I don't talk anymore, though. They stopped talking to me when our mom died. They also stopped talking to our youngest brother, who ended up killing himself last January.

Everyone knows your business. Hell, when I was in high school, I couldn't even go down and buy a bottle of booze at Broadway Liquors because my dad's aunt worked there. He'd get called before I even got home. You couldn't do anything here in the seventies, eighties, and nineties without everyone knowing about it. But I still always felt lucky to have the support from my family, plus so many people had my mom as a teacher and liked her. It was easier for me growing up than it was for a lot of my friends. You always knew that old Rock Springs had your back—at least I did. Going through great times, and then shit times, and then great times again, it was always home.

When people find out I'm gay, in a lot of places, it could've become this awful thing. I would've lived my six months, then I would've been gone. But I had a great support system. I didn't lose one friend. There was no group that told me to get the fuck out of here. I worked my way up at the hospital and ended up getting my master's degree in hospital administration. I was thankful to work around more women than men. I never would've made it in the mines.

It was kind of hard to find people to date, but not really, because we had a solid gay community here. Let me backtrack, though. I got married to my girlfriend right out of high school because that's what you do here. You get married, get a job, have kids, and then you have the little white picket fence and a dog. That didn't work for me. I ended up staying married for one year. Four years later, I was able to say, "This is me. Hi guys." The gay community at the time was amazing. There were plenty of people to associate with, to fraternize with, to do things with, and be able to be me. There were doctors in the community and all kinds of people.

At the same time, I worried a lot about what people were going to say with everyone knowing my family. People automatically say they know you—but they don't actually know you. I grew up knowing a lot of gay people. So I was very lucky and didn't have to worry much about finding people to date. I don't think I could've done things the way I did them if I lived in a bigger city.

I married my husband in 2008. We've been dating since 2000.

The former governor of Wyoming, Dave Freudenthal, and his wife ended up being my good friends because of one of the corporate council boards I sat on. My husband and I went to his inaugural as their personal guests.

STACY: As for Rock Springs being an inclusive place, I would say yes and no. There's very little diversity, at least when I was growing up. I went to high school when *My So-Called Life* was on MTV. People were very slowly starting to feel comfortable identifying as gay. I had a friend who was pretty heavily picked on and bullied. He had a hard time. So now that I think about it, no, I wouldn't say it's a particularly inclusive place, even though it's historically been one of the more liberal places in Wyoming.

DAN SHINEBERG: Junior high and high school were very different experiences for me. Junior high was essentially an extended period of trauma. Since I was eleven, I've known I was going to be a flautist. My mother begged me not to because she knew I was going to get tortured. She let me do it, but she told me what I was in for—and she was right. My mother worked like a dog to get me my first expensive flute. I played it constantly and ended up overplaying it over the years.

I was already 5'11 in junior high, so I looked like the kid who'd been held back three times because I was so much bigger than everybody else. I had wild, curly hair. I was chubby and had thick glasses. I was a walking target. Kids were completely brutal. You're a big, fat Jewish kid, and you're the flute-playing faggot. It was a constant barrage. I had no friends. I had no school support system except for one teacher, Ms. Alexander, who ended up becoming one of my best friends. She knew what I was going through. My mother couldn't stop it. I was becoming severely depressed and self-destructive. Ms. Alexander made her classroom a safe haven for me. She made it an after-school ritual where I'd go and talk about books with her. She's still one of my dearest friends.

I'd always been the fat kid in school. I developed an eating disorder from it. There were a lot of repercussions from getting bullied that followed me. The last relapse I had for my eating disorder was about seven years ago. It still stemmed from being that tall, fat kid in junior high.

High school was when I took the attitude of, "Fuck y'all. I'm gonna do whatever I want." I joined drama club and became more interested in music. I had a group of friends who were also outsiders. We had our clique and supported each other. We were in the plays. I'd developed a chip on my shoulder, and I started fighting back. I'd also grown another couple of inches. I always connected with my English teacher, Mrs. Bedard. She quietly made that connection so kids wouldn't make fun of me. I definitely gave her a run for her money, but she was always there as a safe space.

People weren't verbally abusive to me in high school; it was more behind-the-back. But I was a gay outsider. I didn't come out until my early twenties, even though everyone already knew. It was the elephant in the room with my family. The friends I had were very good to me. I remember there being a separation between most people. They didn't go into my world—and I didn't go into theirs. All these years after high school, I wonder what everyone was going through beneath the surface. You never know for sure.

LAURA: I feel really fortunate because the group of friends I had were so cool. Growing up in the late nineties and early 2000s is when we started to see more people coming out in Rock Springs, but I don't know what it was like before that. It seems like it would've been a dangerous situation.

My friends were cool about it. I didn't tell my family until I was twenty-two. It was at a simmering point for a long time. Eventually it boils over, and you have to make your worlds meet. Otherwise, you're never going to really live.

Most of the people I was friends with in high school are still my friends, or we're still in contact. I feel fortunate in that not a lot of people were out to get me. We held each other close. Now that I'm thirty-four, I see how beneficial it was to have open-minded friends. There were plenty of people who didn't. I also wasn't affiliated with any type of church in Rock Springs that would've come down on me. My social group safeguarded me from my family.

They were the ones I was concerned about because they've been conservative down the line forever.

KATHLEEN: I was in a relationship with another woman for the past three years. In public, I pretended she was my kid's nanny. I felt like I couldn't be honest because people here can be very close-minded. There are people who are accepting and know the world better; but you see the other side, too. There's not a lot of opportunity for people to be different. I know when I struggled with depression, that feeling of being stifled led to my drug use. I felt trapped and always wanted to live somewhere else. I don't know why I didn't. I felt stuck, I guess.

With the suicide rate, I think there are connections to the lack of diversity and how people get stuck in their ways around here. A lot of people feel very isolated, like Rock Springs is all there is. It's often hard to move away because there are such good jobs. But people can get very stagnant. And it's not easy to express yourself.

9

On Fractured Ground

I graduated from high school in 2004 and tried to go to college in Denver, but I dropped out. When I came back to Rock Springs in 2005, the hydraulic fracturing boom had hit. The town and its surrounding areas sit on vast underground stores of natural gas and shale oil. And the mad rush to extract this untapped store of energy upended Rock Springs—once again.

Suddenly every hotel was filled with roughnecks from across the country who were working in the oil field. Rent got a lot more expensive, and stucco neighborhoods sprouted up like an invasive species. Guys with huge work trucks blasted around town. Most of my friends got jobs with Halliburton or one of the other companies doing fracking out in the Jonah field. At the time, we had the biggest Halliburton fracking facility in the country, its massive arsenal of red trucks and heavy-duty equipment on militaristic display. Schlumberger had their own battery of blue trucks and equipment on the other side of town.

Told by people who worked in the oil field, residents who got consumed by drugs, women who had to navigate a town where men outnumbered them ten to one, and others who were there, this is the story of the fracking boom in Rock Springs.

JOE MYER: When you drove through the area at night, all you saw was drilling rigs.

CHRIS SCHMIDT: I worked in the oil field for almost two years. I was a field pump technician for Halliburton. We would fix and rebuild these huge valves that pushed water and chemicals during the fracking process. The pumps were constantly breaking down because they were working twenty-four hours a day. They would take one pump off-line, and, while we fixed that one, they'd put another on the well. So we fixed pumps for fourteen-hour shifts—and oftentimes longer.

We had a shop crew that would work on pumps when they needed to get taken back to the shop. We also had a field crew, which is where I worked. So every day we'd show up at the Halliburton shop at 4:30 a.m. to get on the bus that chartered us all out to the Jonah Field. We'd relieve the crew in the field and then sit in the truck and wait for something to break. Sometimes it was eighteen hours of nonstop hard labor; but then other times there might be like three days when you wouldn't leave the truck. It was usually freezing outside, so you really did not want to get out of the truck.

The whole time I worked out there, I was honestly pretty fucking terrified. My second day, this guy in the shop had this huge water tank lifted up on a forklift, and, instead of strapping it down, he tried to drive really slow. When the tank started to wobble, he got out. It ended up coming down on him and literally ripping his face off: from where his hairline started all the way down to his nose. I was sitting in the shop and heard this horrible scream coming from one of the bay doors. This guy was crawling on his hands and knees with his face hanging off. From that point on, I was terrified to go to work every day. There was inherent danger working with such huge machinery all the time. If one little thing goes wrong at any point in the chain, it can so easily mean instant death.

At that point in my life, I was desperate for money. My parents had paid for me to go to rehab in Montana when I got in trouble, so they didn't want to pay for my college. I wanted to move up in life, and I could make a lot of money fracking. It's funny, everyone out there used to call me Peaches because I was so careful. They'd joke around and say I bruised like a peach—but it was actually because I was so careful all the time. I was always trying to do things the right way and be safe. Someone said, "Why, do you bruise like a peach?" In reality I was still terrified from seeing that guy's face get ripped off.

There was a lot of drug use in the oil field, which is the first time I relapsed after coming back from Montana. The party lifestyle in that line of work is thrown in your face all the time. That was probably the biggest negative for me. The positive side is that it set me up to have a different perspective than people who go straight from high school to college. I had the real-world experience of working eighteen-hour days for two weeks straight and one week off—and I knew that was something I couldn't go back to, because I was so miserable. When I got into college, I was super driven to do it.

School was a huge motivator when I worked at Halliburton. I knew I could pay for my first year. I figured after that I would be able to understand the system of financial aid more and keep going. My mom graduated high school from a homeschool program. My dad never graduated. As a first-generation college student, I didn't know much about that world and how it worked. My parents had zero idea of how to help me apply or register for college, let alone pay for it. They didn't fully understand why I wanted to go to college, because I was making such good money in the oil field. And I totally get it. After getting three degrees and the job I have now, I still make less than I did my first year in the oil field. So when I quit, people thought I was stupid for going to college. I'm grateful that I didn't listen to them, because I saw the long-term game of high-volume fracking not being a sustainable enterprise. My goal when I worked out there was just to get out of Rock Springs.

I did meet some extremely cool people. The hard part was that everyone seemed to carry some kind of weight with them, that thing that was holding them back, whether it was drinking, or a terrible relationship with their wife, or drugs, or just being young and dumb. It seemed like everyone working out there had this hundred-pound demon on their back that was always present in one way or another. We all understood that about each other and respected it—almost to a fault, because we wouldn't call each other out on our bullshit. It was the addict mentality of, "We're in this together, and everything else is bullshit."

ANDREA: I think it was a fairly common perception for people in Rock Springs to see college as a waste of time and money. You could make so much quick cash with those jobs. Once you start making that kind of money, it's hard to stop. I saw this a lot at the high school: kids saying, "Why should I go to college when I can work in the mines or at the power plant?" I knew where they were coming from, because it wasn't too bad when I was working at the salon during the seventies boom and making decent money. But then there were dry spells.

Other kids want some time away from college. I always recommend they at least get a trade. For a lot of the kids who worked in the oil field, they didn't get a trade they could apply outside the oil field. Many of them would do the same stuff over and over again out there. Had they gone to college and taken classes in welding or mechanics, say, they would've set themselves up for the future a bit more. But again, I could always understand why they'd see college the way they did. Especially when you have the cars, trucks, house, and big toys—you have to keep up with the payments, and it's hard to get out of that cycle.

Not a lot of those kids saw that the boom would end.

BRIAN: I was drinking heavily for about eight years while I was working in the oil field and paying for my dad's cancer and all that shit. Unfortunately, I almost drank myself to death. But then I woke up one morning and finally decided to make a shift. I honestly don't think I'd be alive right now if I hadn't left Rock Springs.

As weird as it sounds, I actually really miss my job in the oil field. I was a centrifuge technician. Pretty much all my crew did was related to cleaning drilling equipment and fluid. It wasn't that dangerous for me, unless we were having massive problems with well bores to the point where the rig could burn down, which happened a few times in my career. But for the most part it was real safe. It was hard work but super chill overall. It afforded me a lot of financial independence. Because of the job, I couldn't say goodbye to my dad before he died. It was still a means to an end.

My job broke up the monotony so I wasn't around the same drug people in town all the time. It was a different social climate than most jobs, which I enjoyed. When someone had a problem with you, you'd walk off-site and fight. And then you were good. You'd tell someone to eat a pile of shit if they told you to do something you didn't want to. You'd get fired from any other job if you did that.

The camaraderie from working out there was very real. You'd work with these guys for so fucking long, such long shifts of being out there. If someone started shit with you at the bar, these guys would beat the fuck out of that person. They actually had your back. There were weird drug addicts and shit, but most of the people out there were good people trying to make a living for their families. There was more camaraderie in the oil field than any other job I've had. Even working in oil fields in other states, you end up running into people you met years and years ago [in Wyoming], and it's awesome to see those people.

I'm going to school for HVAC right now. Hopefully I'll get a job in the oil field again, maybe in Texas doing cryogenics. I'm going through the motions of getting my EPA certification. I want to work with my hands. A tech job or something like that wouldn't do it for me.

J.J. ANSELMI: I remember my best friend telling me about some dude who was tweaking and working on a rig. I guess he got caught in the equipment somehow, and it peeled the skin of his arm off—almost all of it. He was super high, so it didn't cause him that much pain at first. He fought against his coworkers when they told him he had to go to the hospital.

NATE MARTIN: Meth is a rural drug, and it's also connected to the oil field. We've all heard the stories of people working these long shifts and hundred-plus-hour weeks with this dangerous equipment—and some of them do meth to help them get through. So some people take it for work reasons, but of course there's a lot of recreational usage as well. The fact that you could cook it yourself made it widely available in places like Rock Springs. It's harder for people to make now since there have been restrictions on some of the ingredients; but it was pervasive at the time. Since the town is isolated, you could just make meth in your trailer or anywhere else. My friend had a trailer on the outskirts of town, and we'd have these raging parties out there. We knew no one would call the cops because the trailers on either side of my friend's were both meth labs.

PETE: Doing meth is like being myself but times ten. You're really excited and love everything, you want to talk with everyone about everything. But then you don't want the buzz to end. It's great and it feels good, but everything goes downhill once you start using the needle. You use that fucking needle and you become a person you never wanted to be.

Injecting it is ridiculous as far as how much it fucks you up. It's like the movies, man. You hit it and it puts you in a completely different world, almost like you're dreaming. I smoked meth for a long time before I injected it. I always thought people were nuts for shooting dope. My buddy who just passed away was actually the first person who hit me with a needle. I fell in love with it.

I moved out of my buddy's house and started doing dope in my house out north of town. When I tried to kill myself, it was all the other shit I was dealing with plus doing dope—so it was all amplified times ten. I was going to work and being generally unstable, doing a bunch of mushrooms and other drugs, too. It doesn't work. Maybe it does if you're good at it, but I wasn't good at it. I was trying to be in a relationship and live life and do drugs at the same time. I sucked at it.

My parents' house got raided for drug shit. My nieces and nephews were there and got taken into custody with the state. We have them back now. It was sad, but it's also like, what did you expect? Everything you thought could happen—it happened. My mom's on probation now.

I'm also on probation because I got caught being a middleman, which I don't regret at all. People say stuff like, "That's fucked up you got caught." But you can't skateboard around town handing drugs off to people and not expect anything bad to happen. I did it for about three years—it was my thing: skateboarding around town and meeting people. I still played in bands and shit, but it was a struggle. Some people do stuff like that and never expect any consequences. There are always consequences.

Someone wore a wire when I got caught. I remember that time-frame but not the person because people were constantly calling me. If you're going to do shit like that, you can't not expect to get busted. It always happens when you least expect it. I actually quit doing it for a while not long before I got caught. I was getting these crazy feelings in my body like I knew something bad was going to happen, and then a week later, something bad happened.

MARY: Back in the day, in the nineties and early 2000s, Rock Springs was a pretty awesome town to grow up in. But when I graduated, it changed because of the boom and the drugs. It went to shit. Nobody cared about anybody else anymore.

Before then, it was a town you could call home. People raised so much money for my brother when he got paralyzed. Everybody knew everybody, and there was a lot of love. There weren't people out to hurt you as much, people who are just out to get whatever they want. People who came in only saw it as a money-making town—and where that could happen really quickly. People from all over were very enticed by that. And then they realized it was a good place to get fucked up and do drugs, and word got out to people who sold drugs. You could make money quickly, rip people off, rob people.

I didn't really start doing drugs until around 2005. I remember going to football games on Friday nights when the whole town would show up. But then drugs, especially OxyContin, took hold of a lot of people. I lost so many friends when OxyContin came around, both losing them to death and just losing people as friends—people who you thought were family but fell in too far. Everybody and their mother did Oxy: lawyers, doctors, all sorts of people doing it behind the scenes. The epidemic was very real. It was crazy how fast things would unravel for people once they started doing OxyContin.

The first time I tried it, I actually threw the other half of the pill out the window because it made me sick. I said I'd never do it again. What felt like a few weeks later, I was fully addicted.

Nobody really knew what it was. We just wanted to do it together, and that was a cool part of Rock Springs: when we tried drugs, we all wanted to experience it together. But when it came to Oxy, we tried it together, and then everyone became greedy and selfish. Suddenly people were willing to steal from you in a heartbeat. You went from being family to being strangers in no time.

Meth was huge, too. I didn't ever do it, but my dad was one of the biggest meth dealers in town. He got sent to federal prison in 2007. That wasn't a drug I wanted to mess with. I was a free spirit, trying mushrooms, acid, and things where I could explore my soul. I'm still all for that type of exploration to this day. But I'm not for the hard drugs like meth and anything else that changes a person's mind and soul for the worse. It can turn people into not-great humans.

I hated meth. I'd lost my mom and didn't even know my dad. He was this huge tweaker who I'd never met. I promised myself I would never do that. I was okay with bud, coke, heroin, and Oxy, but meth seemed like the devil's drug. Meth used to be more of the older generation's drug of choice; but then from 2005 to 2009, it seemed like everybody was on it. A lot of people in the oil field didn't care what they got, as long as it was meth, heroin, or Oxy.

Around 2009, people were paying $200 a pill for OxyContin. That's when a lot of my friends moved to Utah and started doing heroin because it was cheaper and easier to get. And then they would come back to Rock Springs and sell it for outrageous prices. That's when people started switching to heroin. They couldn't afford Oxy anymore.

My brother and I came back in 2009 to sell pills. Two of his best friends tried to rob him. They didn't care that he was paralyzed. People would say they loved him and would never rob him, but then they put masks on and tried to do it.

I've had a lot of friends who OD'd or died: Sean; our old friend from Rock Springs got murdered in Denver by his friend who owed him money for Oxy—we saw him the night before; Jason OD'd on heroin; Zach. There have been so many I can't even remember them all. I've tried to file it all away in the back of my mind and not think about it anymore. So many people died from that epidemic.

JOSH RECKER: There was a point a few years ago when it seemed like every time I logged onto Facebook, someone else I knew from Rock Springs had shot themselves or OD'd. I remember saying to a friend, "People there are dropping like flies."

WALT: Hell, I lived in an old warehouse on Pilot Butte off and on for many years. That whole area was ridiculous. It's the drugs, booze, parties, the shitty bars that are gross but somehow comfortable. It's the whole attitude, the danger, the excitement of that danger. That's the culture.

I was just telling my wife about how a few months after we moved to Rock Springs from mostly safe, calm, and normal Logan, Utah, this drunk woman is pounding on our door late at night. She's yelling after my mom. Something about Pedro and if my mom was sleeping with him. I'm surprised my mom stayed inside. She's a little scary herself. The woman eventually left, but not before hitting our truck. Shortly after, we learned that she found Pedro and apparently murdered him. That's at that warehouse I mentioned.

When Gaviotis' was still there, that street was a carnival of shit all the time. You never knew when you'd walk into a house if some giant dude would be standing on a kitchen counter trying to shoot heroin in his arm. I knew a dealer who got busted when his mom found a massive wad of cash in his laundry. Apparently she didn't really wonder about his tricked-out truck in the driveway until she found the cash. He got busted, and I saw him a week later on the street.

We rented that warehouse until about ten years ago. My dad had an office supply store he started out of our apartment in Logan. He knew the main competition in Rock Springs was crumbling, and that a boom was coming. So that's how I ended up there. He was about to go to prison, and he wanted his parents to run the store. We thought he was going to be in prison for forty years. Good old Utah plea bargains had him back in a year. That was the start of Alpine Office Supply.

We stomped the competition—mainly because they had one sales guy, and he couldn't get his shit together. I feel bad, but I went into sales eventually, and even in my ripped jeans, metal band shirts, and long hair, pulling up in a Chevy Caprice with exhaust that sounded like a Harley and loud music playing, I still took most of his customers. He lost his job. He ended up killing himself after their store closed.

I dabbled in the pills when I hung out with Matt and we had our sad little metal band. We played old Atreyu and punk songs rewritten in drop C. We'd chase Percocets with forties (plural). By then he'd pissed off too many people, so it was mostly us two. When he was injured from his accident, I played guitar. Once he healed, I was on bass until our buddy took over. Then I was on drums. We would get shit-faced, and I'd play until I'd kick my drums over and throw shit. Good times.

MATT LEE: In 2005 I got in a bad car accident. There were a bunch of people partying outside town. Dave was out there, drinking. I asked him if he was sober enough to drive. He said he was good. It was February, and we had this huge bonfire going. There was someone in front of us on that old dirt road; it was completely iced over. Dave was trying to show off. He pulled into this ditch and gunned it. I remember looking at the speedometer and seeing that we were doing ninety. He pulled out of the ditch, and we started fish-tailing. I remember thinking we were going to die.

The next thing I remember is waking up in the University of Utah hospital. I was in a coma for a week and had broken seventeen bones. It took almost nine months to heal. The accident pushed my pain pill addiction, hard. At that time, I had just moved back from Oregon, where I was using heroin. I had been clean for a week before the accident. After, I dove headfirst into pills. I had a prescription for 180 OxyContin eighties a month. I'm surprised I'm still alive—not only from that, but just in general.

JOE MYER: I remember pallet parties out in the woods where dudes were getting guns pointed in their faces. People would set these huge fires in the desert. They were very destructive. I've lived in other places, but none as gnarly as Rock Springs.

JAY ANSELMI: The ratio of men to women was ten to one, or something around there, just like the seventies boom.

KATHLEEN: I remember when I turned twenty-one and started going to the bars. It's more common now for women to be heavily tattooed. At that time, it was still novel here. I had tattoos on my chest with words on them. Guys would be very rude about it. There would be like twenty guys surrounding me and my friend at the bar because we were the only women there. I definitely felt like prey in a way.

Guys would get really mad if you turned them down. I've been called a cunt and everything else by guys I turned down. There's definitely a lot of hunger. Many of those guys were from out of state, so they were only looking for someone to warm them up at night.

My dad always asked me why I didn't settle down with an oil field guy. It wasn't for me. There were so many men, but a lot of the oil field guys seemed kind of the same. They're there for work, and it's all a big money game. They don't care about the place. That's their mentality. It could be scary for sure. Since the guys had a lot of money, they'd want to buy you drinks, then they'd expect things from you afterward.

There are guys who get out of prison and get jobs in the oil field while living in a halfway house or something like that. I've known a lot of them who relapsed. From what I understand, one of the reasons is because they work such long hours. They work seven days a week for sixteen hours a day, and there's the boys' club thing where you crack open beers after a tough shift. If you want to stay wasted, there's meth.

For me, partying just started with drinking. I think my boredom pushed me into the heavier stuff. I wasn't really thinking outside the box, so I ended up going down the path a lot of people here have gone down.

DUDLEY GARDNER: You can look at the Astro Lounge and see it as a continuation of what was happening with the prostitution on K Street in the seventies. It's one of the oldest strip clubs in the country. It's a rocking and rolling place.

STACY: Since the ratio of men to women is so high, I grew up being very comfortable around men, which isn't to say that I didn't have some negative interactions. Sexual harassment and abuse are definitely prevalent there. Women are such a commodity, which made for very different interactions between genders. I never lacked for male attention, that's for sure.

I used to do theater in high school and would do performances at the community college as well. The day I turned eighteen, the Astro Lounge called and asked me to come strip for them. I have no idea how they knew I'd turned eighteen. I remember being in the kitchen of my childhood home in Rock Springs and talking to this guy on our yellow rotary phone. He said he heard I could dance. He offered me $2,000 just to go down there and talk to them. I said, "Fuck no." I think that says a lot about the male/female dynamics in Rock Springs.

Rock Springs was always one of those places where you'd feel on edge and hyperaware of your surroundings. There was always something that could go wrong. It was a tough place to grow up in a lot of ways, especially as a woman. There's something you feel in your body when you come into that town that makes you feel a bit sick. Your body remembers the trauma of what it was like to be there.

J.J. ANSELMI: I went to the Astro on my twenty-first birthday. There were these crowds of what looked like fifteen to twenty guys closing in on every stripper. Everyone had tons of cash, so the drunkenness was completely sloppy and out of control. A few of my female friends experienced some really fucked up trauma at the hands of guys during that time. It's such an aggressive culture. I remember being afraid I'd get my ass kicked pretty much constantly. For a lot of those guys, if they couldn't get laid, they wanted to fight.

Rock Springs had always seemed like a dead end to me. During the boom of the early 2000s, it started to feel very sinister. That's when I started having a lot of suicidal thoughts and developed concrete plans to end my life. I was working a bullshit job for my second cousin, stocking vending machines around town and collecting money from them. My life seemed like a dead end.

LAURA: I worked at a bar and felt like I had the best gig because I got to meet people from all over the place. A lot of those oil field workers were super excited to be making such good money. But man—when it ends, it ends. There's no life. That's when you see the crumbling.

I managed a bar for about eight years. The high ratio of men to women is no joke. There were tons of men during the boom. We were busy on the weeknights because that's when everyone was in town. You'd look around, and there would be eighty to a hundred men, from the higher-ups all the way down to the grunts. We weren't unique in that way. That was every bar you'd go to: just hordes of men. A lot of the service workers were female, which drew a stark contrast.

I was more intimidated by the number of men when I was younger, before I found my voice. You give a few beers to guys who don't know you and there would be a lot of remarks and things like that. But then you do meet genuinely fantastic people. Like any situation, there are going to be plenty of perverted people who want to take advantage; but then there were a lot of people focused on the work, or who were traveling through and had real interest in learning what Rock Springs and Wyoming are all about. I worked at the Outlaw when I was younger, and, from what I've heard, it was similar during the seventies.

There's a lot of extremity. You have these guys who work seventy hours a week. When they're off, they're binge drinking. That's why I left the bar industry in Rock Springs. I did enjoy my job for a long time. I loved booking live music. But looking around, you see how that turns into life for some people. That was a little terrifying. I didn't think I could do it much longer. Some people end up turning the bar scene into their life.

ORLANDO WEBB: When I graduated high school, I worked out in the oil field for different companies. So I saw the boom come and go. I started working there when I was eighteen. That type of labor wasn't my passion or what I wanted to do. I did it because it was good money, and I got benefits and things like that. You have to pay for life somehow. I benefited from the boom in a lot of ways. I used it to help me do other things.

For one company, I was a regular hand. We'd deal with the machinery and the mud. We'd do maintenance on equipment out on the rigs. And then for the other company, I was a pipe cleaner. We'd put up pipes, clean them, inspect them in the shop, then deliver them to different locations. The typical day was to go in, see the work orders, then go out and do the job, whether it was pressure washing or fixing a pipe or cone.

I was never all that scared when I worked out there. Most of my work was on the ground, so we didn't have to climb up the rigs very often. Our crew and company was pretty safe. I was always cautious, but not really afraid. Anything could go wrong at any time. I didn't go out there preparing for something bad to happen, though.

My life hasn't changed all that much since the boom died down. Things have really changed more for people who continued to work in the oil field and made it their career. I make my living as a bartender now, so the change hasn't affected me too much. There were companies that shut down and people who lost their jobs. But that's simply the flow of the economy.

CHRIS SCHMIDT: Being from the millennial generation, I don't think we're a special or unique generation: we reflect a lot of the culture that's always defined Rock Springs. From new mines opening to fracking in the oil field, the entire life of Rock Springs has revolved around a boom cycle that's not sustainable for people who want to make that place home.

ASHLEY: Maybe five to seven years ago there was a boom, but Rock Springs was in a bust phase when I went to junior high and high school. I graduated high school in 2019. My dad works in the oil field, so I'm able to gauge the boom-and-bust cycle based on how much work he has.

To run an oil field operation, you have to invest a lot of money in industry-related expenses to get the insurance, certifications, and equipment, not knowing if you're going to be able to use that equipment again the next year. So I think the boom-and-bust cycles facilitate a constant unease about your financial situation. The culture can become very negative when that's what you and everyone around you are feeling.

CHRIS HAWKS: One of the first things you see when you drive into Rock Springs is a giant billboard about meth and going to jail.

KATHLEEN: If you look at the county jail charges, there's meth charges all over the place. That hasn't changed much over the years.

PETE: Meth is bad this year, man. Plus the heroin and all that shit now. I just lost my good friend to an overdose. I don't know if it was heroin or Suboxone or what. Earlier this year I lost my girl-friend. She overdosed on methadone out of nowhere. She helped me get clean off dope. She'd do Xanax every once in a while because she really was dealing with intense anxiety. It can be so random. People don't realize that Suboxone and methadone can kill you just like heroin. I've known five or six people who've died off that shit. When I think about my buddy, he wouldn't have wanted to go out like that.

J.J. ANSELMI: Those oil and gas companies like Halliburton, Schlumberger, and all the others came to town and put people through the wringer—both physically and psychologically—took the vast majority of the money, and left. They didn't invest back into the community. They played a large part in creating a setting for addiction and suicide to get completely out of control, and then they left the town, with its meagre resources, to deal with it.

JESSE REED: I don't see Rock Springs going through another boom. It will never be like it was, not with the way things are going now. They just closed up some of those places: Halliburton,

Schlumberger, some of the others. I know a lot of people who got laid off. The oil industry isn't looking good right now. We had the biggest Halliburton fracking facility in the country, then they laid everybody off. There's no money in the city budget. I hope it gets better, but I just don't know. I hope something changes. Right now, man, it's scary.

CHRIS POTTER: Halliburton and Schlumberger just abandoned their facilities when they left. They're sitting there, totally empty. It's eerie. There are also a bunch of vacant storefronts in town.

LAURA: There's still pressure for you to get married, buy a $400,000 house, and have a lifted truck and all the toys. You see all your friends with these expensive toys and houses. But what happens if you lose your job? There's no industry to temper that or help people transition and develop new skills. You can't have that life-style and then decide to go work at the post office or something like that. You can't manage those expenses unless you work one of those high-paying energy jobs. There's no way.

When I was in high school, kids who graduated could work in the mines or oil field and make a killing. That's not the case anymore, and we haven't replaced it with anything. What are people looking forward to as far as their career? I think women manage it better because we've had to: women have always thought of multiple careers, like teaching, nursing, getting into banking, or moving somewhere else to see what's out there. Women just don't get paid as much. For men, it's pressurized. You either leave completely and go to school, or do something else, which is fairly unlikely; or you have to go into some type of mining or mineral extraction. What do you do when those jobs aren't there anymore?

10

Out Here on Our Own

Suicide has become an unwelcome fact of life for so many of us. When we consider why suicide rates are so high in the rural West, Rock Springs ticks all the boxes: widespread addiction, a dire lack of mental health resources, tough manual labor, dwindling industries, a culture of rugged individualism, and a shitload of guns. Wyoming currently has the highest per capita suicide rate in the United States. Sweetwater County, where Rock Springs is located, has seen particular devastation.

You can read academic studies and pore over statistics, but there's a gravitational despair in Rock Springs those things don't capture. The area is beautiful in a serrated way, with sharp air and open spaces slicing toward the horizon. You can do whatever you want in the desert, and no one will care. That collective despair, however, is always present, even if it's lurking beneath the surface.

I've known nine people who shot themselves in Rock Springs, one man who killed himself by running his car in a closed garage, and multiple others who overdosed. Since I was a child, people I know and love have been dying by their own hands. It tears holes in your psyche. Everyone I know from there has experience with suicide. Everyone. During the writing of this book, two more of my old friends killed themselves. Something needs to change.

What follows are accounts from people who've felt compelled to take their own life, mixed in with stories from people who've witnessed the devastation suicide causes, both personally and within their community.

PETE: It almost seems like suicide accounts for half the death rate here. It hits so close to home: it's down-the-street-type shit. I'm so used to it by now that it's not much different to me than people passing away from natural causes.

I tried to kill myself three times, man. They put me in a mental institution. People think suicide is selfish, but you never know what someone is thinking at the time, or what they've been through.

The first time I tried it, I was way young, like around eight years old. It scared the fuck out of my parents. The second time I was twenty-six. I tried to jump off the bridge that goes over Bitter Creek and the railroad tracks, that big bridge by the high school. People grabbed me and stopped me before I could do it. I went to the hospital and they asked if I was stable. I just said, "I'm good."

I was still fucking around with my ex, doing dope and shit. They gave me Ambien when I was in the hospital. I took eighteen of those motherfuckers and ran into her house saying shit like, "I'm going to fucking die tonight." That was a crazy time in my life. I never thought I would be that person. They took me to the hospital again, gave me a bunch of liquids, and told me to sleep it off.

WES CARTER: I've known a lot of people who killed themselves. It also depends on your definition of suicide, because I've known a lot of people who OD'd or drank themselves to death.

MIKE: It seems like every year someone from our graduating class dies of suicide or overdose.

ALICIA: Yeah, I've dealt with suicide. There was a suicide in my family.

JAY ANSELMI: I've seen one family member and three of my best friends go out that way. Not that I'm bragging, but it is what it is. Carlos in '95, Mike in 2006, Paul on the first weekend of March 2009, and then Darrel in 2013, on his brother's birthday. Darrel had been sober for thirty years, so it was a big shock. There've been other people I've known from both older and younger generations. Ever since high school, I've been seeing people kill themselves.

J.J. ANSELMI: I loved those guys my dad is talking about. They were such genuine, kind people.

My cousin shot himself in 2009, when I was twenty-four. That one hit me extremely hard. I'd spent a lot of time with Paul when I worked for his vending machine company. We'd hang out at his apartment and get obliterated on pills and vodka. He called my dad multiple times over the years saying he had a gun in his mouth. I remember my dad on the phone saying, "Don't fucking do it, Paul."

LISA SPANJERS: I talked to Paul a couple months before he shot himself. I think he was going back into rehab.

BRIAN: At this point, I've known over fifteen people who killed themselves in Rock Springs. A lot of people in that town self-medicate. Regardless of whether your parents were alcoholics or addicts, the conditioning is different with suicide being around.

MATHIAS: Every year I was in high school, it seems, there was someone who died from suicide. And then when I went to college in Laramie, three students died from suicide the first year I was there. Yet by the time I got to college, that first year of three suicides didn't feel that out of the ordinary. Growing up in Rock Springs had prepared me for it.

The first suicide I remember was when I was in eighth grade. My memory is fuzzy on this, but I remember my mom talking to me about it in the car. The girl's father died from suicide a while before; it wasn't long after that when she decided to use a gun as well. She stayed alive for a few days but didn't end up making it. I remember seeing her sometime before it happened, going for a run with one of her friends, her back turned to us as the two of them took off.

I didn't quite know what it meant to be suicidal when I was first asked the question. I learned in high school. I always kept quiet about it, though, and never admitted the truth to anyone. I was afraid they'd send me to the hospital or lock me up. I had no idea what it meant to have actual mental health support, or that it was possible to learn how to live one's life with semiregular suicidal thoughts. I think experiences like this are far too common in Wyoming, and especially in Rock Springs.

There was a lot of fear and silence around suicide. I do remember that my peers and friends would all talk to one another about it every time we lost someone. That still didn't prevent us from joking around and saying things like, "I'll kill myself if John doesn't shut up," or small comments like that. I now find those sorts of jokes extremely triggering. At the time it seemed like one of the most ordinary things to say.

Access to care and mental health resources are abysmal throughout Wyoming. Simply put, there are not enough providers, even though we do have some amazing mental health professionals who live and work here. Because of this real lack, there are not nearly enough conversations about what mental health even means, or what to do if you or someone you love might be struggling. Similarly, it's so easy to feel isolated in this state, especially if you are a person of color, someone who is queer, or anyone else who doesn't fit the category of stereotypical white, straight, cisgender man. You can't easily receive good care that's culturally competent or sensitive if you're Black, Indigenous, Latinx, queer, or otherwise marginalized.

KATHLEEN: I've been through a lot of trauma. In addition to going to prison, I was in a very toxic relationship for a long time. I'm at a point where I'm working on my mental health. I've looked up resources—it only seems like a lot of dead ends. There's Southwest Counseling, but that's not the route I want to take. And there's not much at all in terms of alternative approaches. It's always interesting to hear from other people about how many resources and routes they have where they live.

I've been through therapeutic treatment here. They basically told me I was a criminal and needed to solve my criminal mindset. Approaches I've heard about in other places seem like they try to get at the root of the problem a lot more. The approach here seems to mask the problem instead of trying to solve it, or really understand it. They throw you on medication, and that's it.

SWEETWATER COUNTY PREVENTION COALITION: My partner and I are prevention specialists, and we're both new here: she started three months ago, and I started two months ago. I'm not sure how long the prevention specialists before us were here. I know the Coalition has been around for a few years, but not too long. When we came in, we had to do some revamping in order to receive the state grant. As the previous leadership was leaving and we were coming in, the structure was kind of falling apart a little bit, so we've been focused on rebuilding. Membership-wise, there are about forty-six people on our email list and another twenty or so who attend our meetings regularly.

I know people want answers from us. We're trying as hard as we can, and we're looking for a lot of those same answers. We live in an age where there are answers for so much right at our fingertips—but then there are still questions about things like suicide and addiction, which have been going on since the beginning of humanity.

Our desks are physically located at Southwest Counseling. We do prevention work for Southwest Counseling, but we're also employed through the state. So we basically wear two hats. We might be a bit partial toward recommending Southwest Counseling because that's where we're housed. We're not necessarily a nonprofit, although we do use a sliding fee scale so cost of treatment isn't a barrier for people.

JACK WATERS: We have next to zero mental health services. We have Southwest Counseling, who seem like their main concern is to make money. I've spent hours upon hours with those people in the emergency room. They've come in after people make actual attempts on their life and said there was nothing wrong. That's one of the things that happened with my little brother. He ended up on a seventy-two-hour hold because he tried to kill himself. He walked out without so much as an appointment with a counselor. I went berserk. Even when you do get in there to see them, it's not the best.

About ten years ago, I was hired as the executive director of the Board of Health in Sweetwater County. I was at a public health workshop in Denver, and they had this map of the Western United States. It was color-coded to show where mental health services are adequate, and where they're not. Sweetwater County was all red. Just glaringly red. People asked me if it was a mistake. I said, "No, it's not a mistake."

So you couple that lack of resources with the boom-and-bust cycle and the general toughness of living here. There's no green. The wind blows. I've had so many doctors and their families land at the airport who planned to work here. They get to the bottom of the stairs, look around, and then get right back on the airplane to fly off into the sunset. They look at Rock Springs and say, "What the fuck is this place?" All these things combine to create a dire lack of mental health services.

It's also tough with the laws in Wyoming. They have Title 25, which is the requirement for a seventy-two-hour hold, similar to the Baker Act. Then they can send you away after that. So you get places like Southwest Counseling that are more concerned with their bottom line than helping people in meaningful and long-lasting ways.

I've had my share of taking care of victims of suicide attempts, let me tell you. When I first worked in the ER in the eighties, we used to hold people for the seventy-two hours and then give them a bus ticket to Evanston or Casper to get out of our hair. But then you had Evanston and Casper buying people bus tickets to send them to Rock Springs. The hospital wouldn't get paid in a lot of those situations because the county was saying it was the state's responsibility to pay—but then you had the state saying it was the county's responsibility to pay. A lot of times, people who got sent elsewhere made homes in those towns in other counties. They didn't want to come back here. From my professional perspective, it's a lot easier and more productive to take care of the same people over and over and get to know them rather than trying to take care of this influx of people you know nothing about. I used to know a lot of the people when they'd walk in the door; but then it got to be someone new all the time.

The other side of the coin is how we're taught to see mental health here. The message is for people to deal with it on their own.

KARA: I haven't been personal friends with anyone who died by suicide. My dad has, though. His younger friend Keith killed himself. That was very intense. My dad was a father figure to him and took him fishing all the time. It seems like the majority of the people who kill themselves in Wyoming are guys, and I think that has to do with the rugged individualism that's valued there. Guys aren't supposed to talk about their emotions. You're supposed to keep moving forward and keep working.

There's a lot of death in addition to suicide, like people dying young in car and motorcycle accidents. Several of my dad's friends got cancer. They all lived that Rock Springs lifestyle.

J.J. ANSELMI: I knew Keith and hung out with him a bunch of times. He used to wear this Clutch *Pure Rock Fury* shirt, which I thought was rad because not a lot of people in Rock Springs knew about Clutch. Keith partied hard and was a pretty gnarly guy. Very tough. I can't imagine Wyoming's macho culture served him well, especially when he was in pain. It definitely didn't serve me well when I was having a lot of suicidal thoughts.

MATHIAS: Wyoming has a "cowboy up" mentality where people are supposed to be stoic and ruggedly individual. When the going gets tough, you're supposed to toughen up. Asking for help is seen as a weakness.

CHRIS SCHMIDT: To be honest, it seems like a lot of people there see mental health as a fairy tale. That's how I was brought up. It was always like, "You have a job, so why are you depressed?" There's this unwillingness to relate to people on an emotional level. I remember being surprised in college when I'd see my friends talk to their old friends. They were so much more emotional. It was surprising to hear guys talk about their feelings. When I moved, I had to really teach myself how to engage in an emotional friendship.

The ideas of masculinity from living there get rooted so deep. You're not supposed to say shit about your feelings, because then you're not a man. I haven't lived there for a long time, and I still catch myself thinking like that. I can't tell you how many times I heard someone say, "Harden the fuck up." Women and men are both expected to adhere to stereotypical gender roles.

SWEETWATER COUNTY PREVENTION COALITION: One of our strategies is called man therapy. The premise is to basically show tough men who've been raised or inundated with the cowboy up mentality that they can seek help with mental health and not be considered less-than because of it. You're not going to be viewed as weak because you're taking care of your mind. In fact, it takes a lot of strength to take that step.

The cowboy up mentality and the idea that you can always pull yourself up by your bootstraps is a big challenge for us. The highest numbers of suicides are for middle-aged men who work in the extraction and construction industries. Men working jobs that put a strain on them physically and mentally end up just continuing to go to work every day and not taking the time to really check in on themselves and their mental health. So that's where we're getting hit the hardest—and it's also the population where you see a lot of that cowboy up, pull-yourself-up-by-your-bootstraps mentality. We're trying to flip the cowboy up phrase into "cowboy strong," which includes taking care of your mental health and not being afraid to seek help.

MATT LEE: When it comes to thoughts of suicide, I've been there while in Rock Springs. I've also been there outside of Rock Springs. I have mental illness: I'm bipolar. But I know that's not the case with everyone who thinks about killing themselves in Rock Springs. I've had several friends from Rock Springs who either died by suicide or drug overdose. It might be a shitty answer, but I think it has a lot to do with how little there is in the way of opportunity. If you feel trapped there, like you don't have any other options, it's easy to get to that place. I've definitely been there, like, "Fuck, this is my life. And if this is what it's going to be, then fuck it. I might as well just end it." I'm obviously glad nothing ever came of those thoughts. They've definitely been there, though. Maybe the everyone-knows-everyone shit has something to do with it, but that's any small town.

If you ever get arrested for anything drug or alcohol related and put in the system in Rock Springs, they try to put you in these mental health programs through Southwest Counseling. That was the only real option for mental health there. I'm sure you could get an independent psychiatrist in Rock Springs, but I never found one, and I'm sure they're pretty fucking expensive. If you tell a doctor there that you're having mental issues, they refer you to go to Southwest Counseling. So there's not any solid psychiatric facilities in place. Southwest Counseling cares more about billing than anything else.

I've dealt with that place a lot through court stuff. For them, it's all about keeping you in their system. When I got arrested in January of 2012 for possession and use of heroin, and possession and use of marijuana, they threw me on probation. Along with that came the IOP program. But I had recently had a friend die by suicide, so I'd had some drinks. I failed a UA for alcohol, and they threw me into rehab. It just felt like a way to keep me in the system. I was doing well right before that. I tried to walk out of rehab twice. My probation officer told me to go back in both times. The second time, I asked her if she could send me to jail instead. I tried to think of a way to get out of rehab without catching more charges, so I went to a doctor and told him about my mental health problems. He gave me a prescription for Valium. I snuck the Valium into rehab and took the entire bottle. I woke up in a jail cell. I don't remember much of it, but I guess I was able to walk and talk to people.

I was in jail for nine months. It was honestly the best thing that could've happened to me. That rehab program was such a joke. You couldn't cuss and could only talk to your family once a week. You had to earn visits with good behavior. But when you're in the throes of withdrawal, you need to see your family. They shouldn't be able to limit that contact. Plus it was all based on this bullshit morality. I truly felt like I was better off in jail. It might not have been the best way to go about it, but fuck them—that's where I was at that point.

ORLANDO WEBB: I've dealt with suicide a few times: my friend, my cousin, a friend in high school. It's there, I've seen it. When a community is tight-knit and close, it can also push outsiders further away. People get clique-y in small towns. One person might start in on someone and then all their friends join in because they want to be part of a clique. But then the person they exclude can start to feel very alone and isolated. It's hard to explain depression and stuff like that to people who've never gone through it—and it's difficult to tell someone how you really feel and what's going on. It can be scary when you're by yourself.

MATHIAS: I was diagnosed with anxiety and depression when I was eleven years old, which is far too young to really understand what those diagnoses even mean, or to be aware of the reasons as to why I was labeled and treated in such a manner. From the moment I was forced to go to a psychiatrist, though, I knew the stigma of going into that building. I was terrified someone would recognize our car driving past, or someone I knew would be in the waiting room.

ANDREA: Sometimes we don't want other people to know we're hurting. We worry they'll think poorly of us.

SWEETWATER COUNTY PREVENTION COALITION: When we promote the Suicide Lifeline and things like that, we make sure to let people know it's completely confidential.

ALICIA: You only have two choices to get help there. People worry they'll run into someone they know, and then that person could violate your personal information by telling a family member or spouse why you're there. Next thing you know, it's all over town. So it's like, "Why would I go to Southwest Counseling? I know four people who work there."

Part of my job is managing counselors for a crisis helpline. Some people just want to talk. Working in mental health the years I have, I can tell you that anonymity is one of the sanctities of our profession. If a person worries they won't get that anonymity, it's likely they won't seek help. People are suffering in silence because of how judgmental that town can be.

They also need to address it more in school and get into the *why* of suicidality, including the social context and possible traumas behind that. People in school never talked to us about where we could reach out. I wish they also taught kids that those thoughts and feelings are nothing to be ashamed of. If you can create a safe space for someone in that moment, things can turn out very differently. I've seen directly how powerful one person's impact can be on someone who's dealing with trauma.

DAN SHINEBERG: One of the things about suicide is that, a lot of times, you have no idea the person is going through such turmoil. There's no amount of training that can help you predict it every time.

MATHIAS: There was only one time I remember anyone coming to talk about mental health in school. I remember a counselor came to talk to my class. It must have been about fourth grade or so. It was a pretty useless conversation. I don't remember much of it.

When I think about how we talked about mental health and suicide at school, I think of the abstinence-only sex education and anti-drug programs, i.e., D.A.R.E. The link here might not seem super direct, but when someone is exposed to these sorts of programs that teach from a supposed sense of morality and scare tactics—and nothing that's actually evidence-based or shown to be effective—there is no safe environment to talk about something like mental health. You can't be vulnerable, especially when mental health is so related to drug use, relationships, and sexual health.

So our approach to suicide and mental health was mostly not to talk about it. That said, I do remember some conversations to the effect of, "Many people think about suicide in their lives at one point or another, so it's not that abnormal." But those conversations, while trying to normalize certain aspects of suicidality, did nothing to teach us about how to get help or support for ourselves, or for people we loved. We were simply never taught how to talk about mental health. We were only taught silence and isolation. Cowboy up.

SWEETWATER COUNTY PREVENTION COALITION: I still hold onto the idea that, with the information we put out, someone who needs it and hasn't said something to someone is really getting something from it.

There's so much that can still be done. The question becomes: how do we make sure what we say is actually going to matter to someone someday? We have to keep doing the long-haul thing by putting the word out there and speaking on a variety of platforms. We're in the middle of trying to change a culture, so it's going to be a lot of work. Things won't be magically fixed tomorrow, or even in ten years; but I think over time we'll start to see a bit of a change.

A lot of it starts with the youth: educating the youth. It's hard to think about your own childhood and what would've made a difference when you were in school. It's also difficult because, sometimes, the parents won't agree with what the kids are learning in school. There's some type of consistency that needs to be in place. Everyone is entitled to their own opinions and beliefs—but with the cowboy up culture, if kids are going home and feeling down, they're going to be less likely to get the help they need if they're constantly being told things like, "You're okay, kid. You'll turn it around. You're just having a bad day." So in addition to educating the youth, it would be so powerful to be able to educate the parents as well. It's hard when you're talking to people who've already been set in their ways for a long time. Does it even make a difference if I talk to them? The answer is probably yes, but it's still an uphill battle. That's a lot of our job, thinking of how to implement ideas and communicate with people in ways that won't push them away. These are the kinds of conversations we have on a regular basis.

LAURA: Rock Springs just had another suicide a couple days ago. It was a young man. The wind and the culture both play into it. Rock Springs has a hardcore culture of defensiveness. People rear up when you look at the negative side. But there are real problems there. The suicide rate is a public health crisis.

Gun culture combined with extreme lifestyles is a recipe for disaster for a lot of people. There are good parts of gun culture, like hunting and being able to sustain yourself that way—but it's also an undeniable part of the high suicide rate. Everyone has guns.

SWEETWATER COUNTY PREVENTION COALITION: Guns aren't the problem in themselves, but rather the way we store them—and having easy access. We talk a lot to people about making sure their guns are stored safely and locked away. Suicidal people with guns are simply much more likely to die by suicide than those without easy access to firearms. People don't live in Wyoming for no reason. They like the independent aspect and want to get away from the hustle and bustle of big cities, so it can be a tough issue to address.

NATE MARTIN: I don't give a shit if you're pro-gun or anti-gun, there's no denying that a lot of people kill themselves by shooting themselves in the head—and a lot of people might not have killed themselves if, during that dark night of the soul, there wasn't a gun within reach. Can you change gun policies to prohibit that from happening? I don't know. But it's simply a factual reality: the preponderance and high availability of guns contributes to the high suicide rate. There's no question. It's such an effective tool for it. Aside from overdosing on drugs, everything else is a bit more difficult. A lot of times it's an impulsive decision, so if you have to figure out which cocktail of pills is going to kill you before your roommate gets home, or the best knot to tie to hang yourself, it might give you a moment to pause and reflect. With a gun, it's only a matter of seconds.

There's also a strong sense in Rock Springs and a lot of places in the rural West that you're really out here on your own. There's not a big social network or a lot of culture for people to attach to and feel like they're part of something. If you become disconnected from whatever connections you have—and I don't think that's very hard or uncommon for people—options can seem few and far between as far as what the future will look like.

JACK WATERS: When my parents died, it was the biggest shocker to me in the world. Because all of a sudden I went from having all my family here—to none.

SWEETWATER COUNTY PREVENTION COALITION: That's what we see a lot: how far community and connectedness can go in preventing suicide. Isolation can be a dangerous pitfall. People need to experience that connection. What we recommend first is to get help when you need it and try to create a community for yourself and a network of people who are going to support you so they might be able to reach out. Studies show that being as direct as possible in those situations is more effective than talking about it indirectly. It's more helpful to straightforwardly ask someone you're worried about if they're experiencing suicidal thoughts and to encourage them to seek help. People often experience more shame when others sort of dance around the issue, asking things like, "You're not thinking of suicide, are you?"

CHRIS SCHMIDT: Yi-Fu Tuan is a humanistic geographer who wrote a book called *Space and Place*. In it, he talks a lot about how physical environments impact peoples' psyches. Rock Springs revolves around a stretch of interstate that runs through it. That's how I felt growing up, like Rock Springs is only a drive-through to get somewhere else. I never felt like I would actually do anything cool with my life. It didn't seem like the world cared about us. I felt like there were no binding elements.

Before I moved away, I knew three people who killed themselves. Of course it was sad, but everyone just attributed it to drugs. That was the scapegoat for suicide. If they found any traces of drugs or alcohol in someone's system, that's how the death would get written off. That became a way for the problem to not seem real, or something connected to the town and environment itself. It seemed less like suicide and more like drug-assisted death.

I first realized the suicide rate there is not a normal thing when I was living in Salt Lake and Facebook became available to people not on college campuses. It seemed like people were constantly killing themselves. Within two years of turning eighteen, I knew something like a dozen people who killed themselves. Seeing it from the perspective of living somewhere else, it really hit home for the first time. I sometimes wonder if that's why people have downplayed what's happening—and has been happening—in Rock Springs: it seems normal when you live there and don't have an outside perspective. And before the internet was around, it was hard for people to truly fathom how isolating a place like Rock Springs could be.

ASHLEY: In fifth grade, I sat in a group with four other students. All of them except for me have killed themselves.

Maybe part of the high suicide rate is the isolating element. You have to drive two hours in any direction to find escape. I also think the stress of the culture here gets passed down to people's kids. Even if everything else is going okay, that economic stress can be enough if you're not getting support. The mental health resources in Rock Springs are spread thin. When local and state governments don't provide that legislative support, they're almost asking for it. When you combine all that with the lack of resources, you create a very dangerous environment for people.

PETE: I went to a mental institution in Lander, which I guess is closed down now. You had two options for that kind of in-patient help in Wyoming: you could go to the behavioral institute in Casper, or you could go to Lander. You're put on a list, and if you don't pass through the first phase, you get sent to the big mental hospital in Evanston.

I took a lot away from my experience there. I try to pass on what I learned when people talk to me about wanting to kill themselves. I've had really close buddies come at me this year who I never would've thought were dealing with that stuff. It's been a crazy year. I try to think about the stuff that caught my ear when I was going through it, like remembering how many people love me. I try to support everyone I really care about. But then some people are so suicidal they won't listen to anybody. It's so easy to dig into hell and just stay there—but you can also learn how to dig into the light and prop yourself up.

I'm on antidepressants; I love them. I've been on Lexapro for six years. It helps me ignore the bullshit. I still get upset, but now I'm able to stop myself from continuing on and on and falling into that hole. It's like the Gojira song, "Gift of Guilt," where he talks about learning how to forgive yourself. You have to embrace the negativity, suffer it, then destroy it. I feel like medication helps me see the person I want to be. It's easy to tell people to toughen up, but that doesn't help when you're in one of those holes. I'm not saying everyone should be on medication. It's helped me, though, and there's no reason to be ashamed of seeking treatment.

You can't just tell people to be happy. You have to be around people who understand where you're coming from. That's really when you'll hear the stuff that catches your ear and sticks with you. I want my life to be calm now. I just want to fall asleep on the couch and shit like that. I haven't been suicidal in a long time. I try to be a lot more cautious.

I have nieces and nephews I take care of, plus my friends' kids. The people in my band are family now. I see their kids every morning at the playground when I drop off my niece and nephew. I love the people who surround me and care about me. I know shit gets hard and shit gets sad. You also have to remember not to bash yourself so much and fall into that trap of thinking you did everything wrong.

11

Phantom Future

As with every mining town in America, Rock Springs faces a deeply uncertain future. Will the town ever move beyond a boom-bust economy? What will happen to Rock Springs as demand for coal continues to plummet? What are people going to do?

CHELSEA: It's hard to imagine what Rock Springs will look like in a hundred years. It's so dependent on oil and fuel resources like that, but those things aren't infinite. And it's not a place that shifts much. They're not looking for what's next.

KARA: I do wonder if Rock Springs would ever become a ghost town. Maybe it wouldn't deteriorate that far, but I think it's going to wither more as the coal industry fades away. I can see all those new subdivisions going vacant and people staying in the older neighborhoods.

LES GEORGIS: Power plants are transitioning to natural gas, and that will be the death knell for electric power from coal, and any coal mines. You don't have the cost of mining or transportation. You build a pipeline, ship it in, and that's that. It will be the death knell for the Jim Bridger plant and mine as well. Point of Rocks has their bar out there. It will most likely fold when the power plant closes.

It's the same problem at Wamsutter. I don't know how many people actually work at that plant. I can't imagine what will happen to it.

J.J. ANSELMI: PacifiCorp recently released a phased shut-down plan for the Jim Bridger plant and mine. My friend who works at Black Butte Coal told me things are slowing down out there, too. Those are two of the main employers for the area.

LAURA: It would be awesome to see more emphasis on going to college and life beyond the mine or working in the oil field. Those are the things the town is founded on, so it's hard. But those things have become thorns in the town's side. I've heard rumors that the power plant is closing. My dad worked in coal—it's what we do. We would take tours out there as kids. You'd get this little black rock candy and a hammer. It's cool when you're a kid but seems kind of weird and dark when you're an adult.

There have been people who try to push Wyoming toward renewable energy. Before he left office, Governor Matt Mead proposed plans for economic development outside of mineral extraction because he could see the writing on the wall with coal. But not many people got on board. He was trying to supplement Wyoming's economy and help the state *before* all the mines and coal industry crumbled. Unfortunately, soon after he left office, mines in Gillette and Kemmerer closed, and it nearly happened in Rock Springs.

In 2016 a lot of people dug in their heels and kept all their eggs in the coal basket. But unfortunately a politician doesn't dictate the market—demand does. So if they had actually begun to supplement Wyoming's economy, I'd have more optimism. I feel like we've gone backwards. People here have doubled-down on mineral extraction. Who knows how the pandemic will affect all this. Some of those oil, gas, and coal companies have used COVID-19 as an excuse to leave Wyoming, but I think they were on their way out anyway.

It's inevitable that Rock Springs is going to have to focus on something else. Things are going to have to change. You can't sustain a town of twenty thousand people where half the population is depending on mines that are probably going under; and then there's also everyone in Green River depending on those same jobs. What are you going to do when so many people rely on these mines?

NATE MARTIN: There doesn't seem to be any appetite at all as far as a concerted effort to diversify the state's economy. There are people working on it, but it's going to be hard. It already is hard. Rock Springs has a few other things going for it—the trona mines most notably. Right now the state is trying to execute this land deal where they're going to buy a bunch of land that's rich in trona and try to mine it. It honestly sounds insane and completely stupid, especially since the economy is getting destroyed by the pandemic.

But what will happen to Rock Springs? It's going to shrink. It's going to become quiet. I grew up during a bust. The boom that brought my parents to Rock Springs was long over by the time I was coming of age. It didn't boom again until the year I left. My whole experience of the town is during a bust period, and that's what it's entering into again. But the difference now is that there's not a boom on the other side of this bust. Coal is not coming back. Natural gas is abundant and cheap, so it's not going to be the moneymaker it once was. People are moving away from fossil fuels in general.

There's going to be a very serious reckoning facing Rock Springs in terms of, "Who do we want to be? What do we want to be? What kind of town do we want?" But I think a lot of people in Rock Springs ignore those types of questions. They latch onto the economy that's there—the jobs that are there—and they ride it like a horse. You have the stereotype of the rugged individual that's prevalent here in Wyoming, but in reality the Western mining town has no control over its own fate. The place hasn't grappled with questions of its own identity outside of protecting the tenuous economic opportunities that may exist at any given moment.

CHRIS HAWKS: I remember driving through not long ago and looking at this hill that they had strip-mined. The landscape was totally different. Flying over it going from Salt Lake to Denver, you could see the coal seams. The amount of earth they'd moved was absolutely staggering.

DANELLE: My mom works at Black Butte Coal as the business manager, and my dad works out there, too, as a truck driver.

NATALIE: I worked in the open pit mine at Jim Bridger. I worked as a glorified shop hand and then on the production line, which was extremely tedious.

I had an interview to work underground at Black Butte, but it made me feel claustrophobic to be down there. It's barely wide enough to drive a pickup through. There's a lot of groundwater, which I didn't know going in. I was wearing my steel toes, but most people wear waders. The water went up to the top of my boots—and yeah, it was pretty cold. The temperature stays around thirty-five degrees in that mine.

I work in one of the trona mines now. Basically, you get all your gear on, including a respirator that can let you breathe for about an hour if there's carbon dioxide in the air. You go down, and thankfully it's wider than the coal mines, and it stays about sixty-five degrees down there. It's easy to forget that you're eight hundred feet underground. I go to my work table and wait for my boss to come out of his morning meeting to let me know what needs to get done.

There's sexism for sure, just like anywhere else. Out of two hundred or so workers down in the mine, there are about a dozen women. Some of the guys make jokes and whatnot. For the most part, though, they try to behave themselves. Honestly, there are also women who like to play the girl card to get out of doing some of the harder work. I mean, I get that guys are physically stronger, and the work can get demanding. That said, I want to work around people who all carry their weight. I tell my wife about it all the time.

For the most part, it's a good bunch. I just make sure not to talk about politics. My boss is liberal, too, and he's a lot more outspoken about it, so he'll get into arguments with the other guys. It's mostly conservative out there, for sure. You're not going to change anyone's mind, so I tend to avoid those arguments.

Two union organizations have approached us, but, right now, we're not unionized. When one union was talking to us, our company basically said they'd give us the money we would've paid in dues as bonuses. Of course that never happened.

There have been two fatalities at our mine. I've seen a bunch of injuries over the years—mostly crushed fingers. One guy got parts of his fingers cut off. This one time, I was installing a J hook to hold up this big pipe. A 120-pound slab ended up falling on my head. We were positioned near the hook. I'm lucky we were up there and not on the ground. That thing could've killed me. You'd like to think your last words would be something eloquent, but mine would've been, "Motherfucker, bitch, goddamnit, bullshit," just this string of cussing.

Trona is used in a bunch of stuff, from Pyrex, glass, and baking soda to all kinds of other products. These jobs pay really well, so it's easy to get used to a certain lifestyle with being able to buy a house and having enough money to buy all the toys and do cool stuff with your family. I probably would've moved somewhere else if it wasn't for that and wanting to be close to my parents in case they need any help.

12

What We've Learned from the Sagebrush

Three years from now, I'll have spent as much time living outside of Rock Springs as I did in the town. But I'll never think of anywhere else as home—not in the same way, at least. When I feel nostalgia for the place where I grew up, it's almost invariably a longing for the desert, a longing to be able to drive ten minutes in any direction and be completely alone.

Over the years, I've found myself feeling more and more protective of that sparse landscape, especially when people say it's ugly. Through the right eyes, it's striking. The harshness of the climate makes it so only the toughest vegetation—mostly sagebrush and cedar trees—can survive. I think of those who live in Rock Springs, or have lived there, in the same way. I may never be a resident of the town again, but I would never want to be from anywhere else.

When I was conducting interviews for this book, the last question I asked people was what living in Rock Springs had instilled within them, what it taught them about life. This is what they said.

MATHIAS: The thing about rurality is that, for those who haven't grown up in these spaces or spent much time in them, it's easy to further marginalize those who do live here. We have an urban/rural divide that privileges and centers urban culture and urban experiences. It's also complicated by my queerness, in that there's the constant notion that I shouldn't be here in Wyoming. We have so few queer narratives in this state—and the one that immediately comes to mind for most is Matthew Shepard—that it's easy to buy into the idea that I have to go somewhere urban to be authentic or to find happiness. So it's hard to acknowledge the real challenges of rurality without further demeaning these places and the people who live here.

For me, Rock Springs is like a thousand pieces of shattered glass. There's not a good way to hold it in my heart or mind without cutting myself. When I tell people about the town, "complicated" is my usual, quick answer. That, or "layered." Both of which are really just code for trauma. I've also many times said something like, "I love the desert. The town . . . not so much. They do have a pretty good community college, though, right?"

The Red Desert is beautiful. I can't describe how I feel about it, other than to acknowledge that part of my soul is still there, in the land around Rock Springs. It's in White Mountain, it's in Adobe Town, it's with the wild horses. It's in the land that I relentlessly mountain biked through. It's desert that I love endlessly because it expanded wide enough to be able to hold all of my pain. I never had to give it any sort of answer as to who I was. The desert is what I think of when I'm tasked with visualizing what it means to come home.

JIMMY: Kids in Rock Springs are really free-ranging. That's how you're raised. You can jump out of your garage with your four-wheeler, and you have some of the best trail riding in the world. You can't do stuff like that in the city. You have to haul your stuff on a trailer or take it to a designated area. We're not as supervised as city folk.

WALT: I used to love going out past the wild horse corrals to the old Lincoln Mine. I don't know if you're familiar with it, but it's where Rock Springs used to be back in the old days. Then they moved it to the area around Pilot Butte and Bitter Creek. Me and a buddy would smoke weed at the old Lincoln mine and look for marbles and shirt buttons. They were basically slobs and left tons of late 1800s/early 1900s litter, including a mound of rotting handmade shoes. There's nothing there now but litter, some foundations, and broken glass everywhere.

We also hiked around a similar place on the mountain behind the Monsanto plant. Each place had garbage dumps from different eras. The one behind Monsanto had a weird baseball-sized hole in the ground. You could drop a rock in and you'd hear it fall for a crazy amount of time. I was out there one day and saw what I thought was a big crazy bug, and I was going to snatch it up with my bare hand. I slowly got closer until I was like ten inches away. I was concentrating like Bruce Lee getting ready to strike when it saw me and whipped its little scorpion tail at me. I realized I needed glasses and didn't try to catch weird bugs after that.

That desert is full of cool shit. I even got shot at out there.

MIKE: I didn't see a lot of beauty in the geography of the place when I was growing up, but I'm starting to now. There's always two sides of the coin, and you have to unwind some of the resentment and anger. I try to own it now. I'm not from Colorado. I'm from Rock Springs. My family has lived there for four generations.

BRIAN: I can genuinely say that I enjoyed fishing and being outside there, even if it was such a negative place. Being an outdoorsman is still a huge portion of my life and who I am. I'm proud of the fact that I could get dropped in the middle of nowhere with a knife and just a few other things, and I'd be perfectly fine. That aspect of growing up there has been a positive and lasting part of my life. Fishing and kayaking are still big passions for me, and that came from living there, when you have literally nothing else to do but go fishing or get fucked up. The music scene there sucked. We tried to make it as good as it could be. It was just very limited. Every band and musician was driving through on I-80, but no one stopped to play shows. I remember seeing Method Man in the C-Store at like five in the morning. That was pretty weird.

ASHLEY: When I think about graduating from college, I'd really like to move someplace where I won't have to fight for certain political things all the time. On the other hand, it would suck to not be able to show my kids the sand dunes and where I grew up. When people paint this picture of Wyoming of all the young people leaving but all the old people staying, I think they take those things for granted.

With all the COVID-19 craziness happening, we loaded up our four-wheelers and went to the sand dunes. It was so cool to be able to do that and not have to worry about seeing any other people. Rock Springs is very geographically unique. Even though it's desert with antelope, sagebrush, and not much else, you can see the beauty of it when everything is green in the spring, or when it's snowy. That's stuff you have to come to appreciate. It's not as immediately beautiful as a place like Jackson. Everyone thinks there are places prettier than Rock Springs. But taking that Rock Springs exit off the freeway after being somewhere else has a lot of familiarity and comfort that people don't realize.

KATHLEEN: I always talk about going to prison in California because it's one of the times I was able to be around a lot of people who weren't from Rock Springs, and where I encountered a lot of different personalities and backgrounds. There were a lot of people who grew up on the streets in cities and had never gotten to experience things like going to a bonfire, or sitting on a back porch somewhere without pollution and looking at the sunset. There's a lot of drug use here, but the violence isn't nearly as bad as other places.

People might not think of Rock Springs as a pretty place. It really is, though. The open spaces are so unique. There are also cool people here—they're just not always easy to find.

There are positive things happening, like the urban renewal agency. They're trying hard to renew downtown and get people to shop local. I know it's easier to go to Goodwill or Walmart or order stuff on Amazon, so it's not always easy to convince people why they should support local businesses instead of those bigger companies. Once people start going to the smaller stores, I think they're often pleasantly surprised at what they have to offer.

When I first came back to town, I was working housekeeping at the hospital. That's not something I wanted to do. There's not a lot of options here for women as far as getting a good job, unless you're educated. That pushed me to start my own business. Not that women can't work in the oil field or mines—but it's uncommon. Since there are so many men, you'd have to be really tough as a woman to work out there. There's a lot of the boys-will-be-boys culture. Unless you're a man's man, it's probably not the job for you.

Since I started my own business, I look forward to coming to work every day. It can be scary because you never know if you're going to make enough money. But I couldn't pass on being my own boss. When you have family and kids here, it can be challenging to move somewhere else if you don't know anyone there. I've learned to make the best of it.

ORLANDO WEBB: Rock Springs is a small, hometown community. It's a place where you don't have to lock your door at night. It's a place where you can raise a family. It's also a tight-knit community where everybody knows everybody else who was raised here. It's a getaway from big city life, for sure.

For the most part, people here have each other's back. It's also like any other town or city where you have your cliques and social circles. But a lot of those circles overlap because of cousins, relatives, and friends having some connection in common.

We always had good times growing up. Our generation plays video games and stuff, but we still got outdoors and spent a lot of time four-wheeling, playing night games, playing sports, and doing all kinds of other stuff. I had a pretty typical childhood here with my friends and family. There were always ups and downs, but unlike a big city, my parents didn't have to worry about me joining a gang or walking home with new shoes on and getting mugged, or shot, or anything like that. It was also a different time because we didn't have cell phones. Kids stayed out playing under the streetlights. We didn't have the constant connection of social media, so our parents weren't able to know where we were at all times. There was the trust to let us go out, play, and grow up. We'd get into trouble, but it seems like nowadays you have to worry more about kids being out by themselves. I think it was easier to be a kid, as much as you can say that with still going through teenage angst and all that.

My mother passed away, but she came from Memphis, Tennessee, and raised five boys on her own. The man I call my father adopted me at a young age. That's the reason I'm here. So I would definitely say there are a lot of very resilient and strong people in Rock Springs. A lot of my family and friends are extremely strong people. That's where I learned strength.

DANELLE: Even though I've seen a lot of racism here, I still think it's a good place to raise kids. Everybody knows everybody, so they end up watching out for each other. Everyone's on the lookout for your kids. I really enjoy that aspect of living here.

JIMMY: The whole community raised you. That's what I loved about Rock Springs the most. No matter what side of town you're from, you know people from every neighborhood. There's a lot of emphasis on knowing your neighbors. My friends' moms became my second moms. There was a lot of support. People in Rock Springs look out for their own. You might fistfight a kid at the other junior high on a Friday night, but the next night at the football game against another town, you're all on the same team.

It's also nice to be more of a big fish in a small pond where people know who you are. You know everybody and can call favors in. If you need to move a couch or whatever, it's not hard to find someone to help you out.

JESSE REED: After working at the Stansbury mine, I worked for DeBarnardi's Construction for about thirteen or fourteen years. I like to joke that I've built about half the town. I did a lot of concrete work: road construction, gutters, curbs, all kinds of stuff. I work for the Parks Department now. I've been there almost twelve years.

Rock Springs is home. I've been here all my life, except for a short time when I lived in Seattle and then came back. But it's home. Everyone knows you. You can't go somewhere without someone knowing you, whether it's the grocery store or anywhere else. I have a lot to be thankful for.

RAY SILVESTRI: When I've gone back to Rock Springs for funerals over the years, I'm always amazed by how many people show up. That town was always very locked together.

JACK WATERS: I have such a real sense of family here, and I don't mean just my blood relatives. We knew our neighbors. We did things with our neighbors. Hell, we'd blast our skateboards down the street without helmets all the time. I wouldn't trade growing up here for anything. There are all these people who can't wait to get out of here, but I think they often take what they have for granted. Once you leave, you realize how unique Rock Springs is.

The old Superior mining community was so tight. It's hard for people to imagine how tight it was. If you were from old Superior, you had it made because those people would give you the shirt off their backs. Same thing goes for people from Rock Springs. I've never seen more charitable people in my life. All you have to look at is when someone dies: the food, the money—my god. People take care of people, and that's old Rock Springs. But I think if I was growing up here now, I would feel differently. That sense of community isn't here as much anymore because a lot of those older residents have died off.

My grandpa was the deputy state mine inspector under Dan Hathaway, the governor. Dan and my grandpa were great friends. I traveled all over the place with my grandpa. I got to know Wyoming and its history. I got to know its people. A lot of people didn't have that. I was so lucky to have family that were cool with me being me. It could've been total hell if it hadn't been like that.

DAN SHINEBERG: My grandparents were street angels. My grandpa owned a pawn shop. My grandparents didn't care about stigmas against drug culture. They just wanted to help people. In the sixties, before the big boom happened, a bus of hippies came through town. This was when my grandparents owned Shineberg's Cleaners. The hippies asked if they could do laundry there. My grandma invited the entire busload of hippies and their kids over to the house to do laundry and shower. The hippies hung out, smoked pot, and did their thing.

My grandparents were just like that. Grandpa was good friends with a guy who got sent to prison for possession and sale of crack. The guy had served his time and gotten out of jail. Grandpa invited him over for Thanksgiving dinner. When I asked my mom if we were going over there, she said, "No. The reason he was in prison was because he broke parole, and I was his parole officer." She called my grandfather, pissed that he'd invited one of her parolees to Thanksgiving. Grandpa said he'd already paid his debt to society, that you have to be good to people.

Whenever I went into my grandpa's pawn shop, people would tell me I looked like my mother. When I asked how they knew her, they'd say, "She was my favorite probation officer." My grandfather loved to be around and help people. It made him feel needed. My grandmother loved hearing people's stories of why they did what they did. She had such empathy for that community. She was a pre-Holocaust survivor. She'd grown up in Germany and knew what discrimination is. She'd watched people get physically hurt for who they were. It had a profound effect on her and how she viewed people.

TAMMY CURTIS MORLEY: My dad ran the pool hall, but he was also the guy who would help people when they needed it. My mom was so ticked off one time because he brought this guy home to die in our upstairs bedroom. The guy didn't have any family.

Dad would also bring home strangers for Thanksgiving and Christmas to make sure they got something to eat. One night this woman came over and knocked on the door. She told my dad that her husband had just gambled off all their money. She didn't have money for food for the kids or the house payment. My dad always wore bib overalls, and he'd carry a wad of money in the pocket. He pulled out the money and just gave it to her. What's funny is that she ended up being his nurse at the hospital when he was dying of cancer.

MARY: Rock Springs taught me to be humble. It doesn't matter if you have money or you're broke. Money doesn't buy happiness, and no one is better than anyone else because of the money they have. I've been friends with people who were rich and people who were dirt poor. You have to see and treat people like they're equals. A lot of people treated me that way in Rock Springs, so that's how I try to be. We knew people with mental problems, or kids who didn't get to eat dinner every night, or kids who were distant because their parents were beating them. Living there makes you humble, and you learn not to judge a book by its cover. You never know what people are dealing with, or what they've gone through. Just because you have money or whatever materialistic shit doesn't make you a good person. You have to treat everyone with love and respect. Being a good person means being kind when no one is looking.

MARCIA HENSLEY: I felt liberated in Rock Springs. I met some of the most interesting people, probably because I was teaching at the community college. The faculty were from everywhere. There were people who'd taught in the Peace Corps, and people with PhDs who could've taught anywhere they wanted to—but because of the outdoor recreation in the area and nearby, like hiking and skiing, they wanted to be in Wyoming. There were these great archaeologists and geologists who opened my eyes to a landscape and lifestyle that, to me, was much less confining than Tulsa, Oklahoma, where I grew up. Tulsa is in the Bible Belt, and the expectations for how to live your life felt more rigid there. In Rock Springs, you had this great mix of intellectuals, blue-collar workers, miners, ranchers, and farmers. I was very taken with the landscape, even though a lot of people think it's ugly. I fell in love with that high desert country. I loved that you could see so far. The air is so clear. I didn't like the dust storms or wind, but, on the whole, I felt the landscape to be empowering.

MIKE: Rock Springs's overemphasis on being self-sustaining caused a lot of resentment, and it can be very dangerous and problematic to people; but I also learned how to be independent early on. Now

I'm trying to learn how to allow myself to rely on other people. It's a double-edged sword.

I held down a thirty-hour-per-week job throughout high school and have been on my own since I was eighteen. A lot of my peers have gone back and forth between living at home and living on their own. There's nothing wrong with that of course, but Rock Springs taught me to be a very independent and self-sustaining person. The beautiful side of that is that it eventually created self-love and acceptance, which ties into being queer. Some people go their entire lives without ever loving that part of themselves. Somehow, I came out of that culture of self-sufficiency with the audacity to accept myself and persevere—but again, I'm still trying to unlearn the toxic elements of it. Trying to move beyond resentment, I try to pick and choose things from the place I grew up and the faith I was raised in that can serve me in positive ways.

ASHLEY: I did the school safety walkout after Parkland, and it was a real learning experience. There was no foundation of activism for me to build on here. When you live in a small town, you have a lot of opportunities to create something for yourself and give back to your community. I think I'll carry that with me for a long time. Having that ambition and drive to do things for yourself can be very powerful.

GLEN HOOPER: People I know now are always surprised when I tell them about Rock Springs. There are times, after it rains, when I really miss the smell of sagebrush. I know the wind can be hard to deal with in Wyoming. It also keeps things moving and in motion. The wind comes up a lot in my music as a presence and its own character.

About once a year, I go camping out south of Rock Springs and just try to absorb the desert. There's a book called *The Solace of Open Spaces* that hits on the calm and solitude you can find in Wyoming. Living there teaches you to be alone, to be comfortable with your own thoughts.

When we used to ride our bikes from our friend's house way outside town all the way to the dirt jumps on the complete other end of town; or when we'd build jumps in a random clearing in the desert; or just go out in the desert and build forts with scrap wood; or catch lizards and horned toads when we were little kids—where else can you do shit like that?

DUDLEY GARDNER: A lot of people don't see the beauty here. They see it and want to leave, which is fine, because they can leave on the same road they came in on. One of the problems with the oil field is that all the workers come in for work and don't want to stay. They want to make their money and go back home where they think it's prettier.

You really have to learn to appreciate open space. Right now, we have so few of them—places where you can find solace in the quiet. But I think people from out of town would see the beauty if they spent time actually walking on the ground in this area. You have to spend time outside, looking at the landscape and the plants that grow here. The oil field workers don't always see or appreciate the birds and wildlife, or the far-reaching horizons. All you need to do is drive south a bit on Highway 430 and get out and walk.

The wind is also hard for people to deal with. But I've worked in Mongolia and other places where the wind is seen as a good thing. It purifies the air, drives away insects, and provides a fresh start. That's not a perspective a lot of people have. Midday during a windstorm or snowstorm can be hard. They say you're either freezing to death or getting blasted to death by the wind—but you can shift that perspective. To me, that's simply not the case. Rock Springs and the area around it is as beautiful as anywhere else.

People always say, "If you can make it in New York, you can make it anywhere." Well, if you can make it in Rock Springs, you can *really* make it anywhere. Samuel Western said the reason people from Wyoming do so well when they leave is because they've learned how to get by with so little for so long. Rock Springs has taught me that in spades—to make use of everything that's provided to me, and to make opportunities where others might not see them.

WING LEW: I could honestly live anywhere and be happy, whether it's Rock Springs or downtown Manhattan.

NATE MARTIN: I can't imagine being from anywhere else, and I'm glad to have it as part of my life. It's a very interesting place. When I went off to college, everyone I knew was from the suburbs. But Rock Springs is a distinct and tough place. I think it breeds tough people. And it's a beautiful place.

I work on the school board in Laramie. The community and various government agencies are trying to buy this plot of land, and the school board is looking at the outdoor educational opportunities for it. Right now, a lot of kids in public schools get sent up to Teton Science School in Jackson for outdoor education. And that's the classic sentiment: the Tetons are beautiful; Yellowstone is amazing—that's the real wilderness and outdoors. But one of my things is that you should expose kids at a young age to the cool aspects of the outdoors right in their backyard. I think about Rock Springs a lot during those conversations. When I was growing up there, no one told me that the Red Desert is beautiful. That's something I learned on my own. It's such an incredible place. I've come to deeply appreciate it as a unique and aesthetically magnificent landscape.

I'm also much more conscious now of the concept of public land. Growing up, I don't remember people saying that you need to keep public lands in public hands. But Rock Springs is surrounded by public land. My conception when I was young was that you had town, where there were rules and police and authority figures—and then you went outside of town, where it was the freedom zone, where you could ride your bike or four-wheeler, or shoot guns, or have a bonfire, or just do reckless fun things without anyone bothering you. A lot of young people grow up without that outlet, without the type of freedom public land affords you.

I lived in Rock Springs again briefly after college, and I got a job with the newspaper. I was covering a meeting where they were talking about drilling for oil and gas near Adobe Town. There was your typical opposition where you had the oil and gas people like, "Yeah, we should drill!" And then you had the environmentalist people saying, "No, we should protect it!" In the middle of it all, this guy stands up and says he has the strangest story about Adobe

Town. He started talking about how, during the 1990s, there was a counterterrorism conference for law enforcement up in Jackson. This was pre-9/11, so not a lot of people in the United States had experience with terrorism or counterterrorism. They needed a keynote speaker. Someone had learned that some guy was friends with a general from the Middle East, and they ended up getting the general as the keynote speaker. But he had a stipulation for doing it: he would only come to Wyoming if he could meet the governor. So this guy who was talking described giving the general a ride from Jackson to Cheyenne after the conference. Along the way on I-80, they looked to the south and saw wild horses. The general asked who they belonged to, and the guy said, "They're wild horses. They don't belong to anyone." That blew the general's mind. The general asked, "Well, who owns that land out there?" And the guy said, "No one. It's public land."

The general's curiosity was piqued, so the driver decided to show him Adobe Town. They got out to Skull Rim and parked along it. The general got out and was completely awestruck looking at this beautiful place, this hard place. He said, "It's places like this where Jesus and Mohammed came to be: this type of austere, desert landscape." He went on to say that places like Yellowstone were like Disneyland, but places like the desert contain this deeper beauty, this more profound beauty.

I've always thought about the Red Desert in those terms. You get engulfed in silence and the space of it—the vastness of the space, where so much of what you're experiencing is just the hugeness of the sky. I also love all the wildlife: the deer, elk, antelope, bobcats, and mountain lions.

GLEN HOOPER: Have you seen the show, *Yellowstone*? Everyone in the family gets a Y branded on them. That's how I feel about being from Rock Springs, like you have this badass scar that really means something.

STACY: Toughness and resilience is in the DNA of Rock Springs. It's connected to the landscape, the terrain, the type of people that live there, the industry that's so predominant there, the boom-bust pace of the mining industry, and the people who are drawn to those industries. It's windy, dirty, and dusty, but if you go out north of town, or to Flaming Gorge, or drive between Rock Springs and Green River when the light is hitting the mesas and plateaus in just the right way, it's also very beautiful. Rock Springs itself just looks resilient in the way it's been formed and how it continues to survive. That becomes part of your fiber when you live there.

ALICIA: I was assaulted twice, both times by people I knew. I'm also a survivor of domestic violence. So coupled with overcoming bullying in Rock Springs, I'm resilient as fuck. Living in Wyoming definitely contributed to that. One of the reasons I'm so outspoken now is because I know what it means for someone to try to take your voice, to try to silence your voice. I don't put up with people's bullshit anymore. I don't have time for it.

MATHIAS: Rock Springs is a place that endlessly fascinates and endlessly hurts me. It's layered like desert shale, which breaks easily.

Acknowledgments

First and foremost, I would like to thank everyone I interviewed for this book. I learned so much from hearing your stories, and I think that will be the case for anyone who reads this. Your experiences paint a portrait of Rock Springs and Wyoming that's more accurate, complex, and profound than anything I ever could have produced on my own. Thank you for your honesty and bravery.

Heartfelt thanks to Jordan Utley for capturing the true spirit of Rock Springs in your stunning photographs. Your talent is humbling.

Thanks so much to my wonderfully brilliant wife, Remy, and to our daughter, Stevie Rose, for your overwhelming love and support. You both inspire me endlessly. I'm so lucky to have you in my life.

Thanks to Grandpa Leighton and Mom for showing me the value and power of storytelling. Thanks to the rest of my amazing family for your undying love, support, and encouragement.

Hearty thanks to Clark Whitehorn and the Bison Books / University of Nebraska Press team for believing in this book and genuinely caring about the West. Your insight has been a gift.

Endless gratitude to Sweetwater County Historical Museum and Debbie Maljian for the permission to reprint excerpts from Thomas Cullen and Marilyn Nesbit's amazing books. Thanks also to *Rocket Miner* (www.rocketminer.com) for the permission to reprint Louis Julius's mine cave-in story.

Special thanks to Ryu Spaeth and the *New Republic* for putting the fracking chapter into the world—and for the invaluable editorial insight. Your feedback ended up having a large impact on this book as a whole, and I'm very grateful.

Finally, thanks to my badass friends for the continued inspiration.

Notes

Most of this book's content comes from interviews the author conducted remotely from March to September 2020. In order of appearance, the interviewees included (quotation marks indicate a pseudonym): Dan Shineberg, "Walt," Nate Martin, Dudley Gardner, Les Georgis, Ray Silvestri, Jack Waters, Wing Lew, "Joan," Jesse Reed, Marcia Hensley, Jay Anselmi, "Alicia," Chris Schmidt, Stephanie Wessel Anselmi, Lisa Spanjers, Tammy Curtis Morley, "Laura," Ginny Spain, "Andrea," "DaNelle," Orlando Webb, "Jimmy," Chris Hawks, "Kara," "Ashley," "Stacy," "Kathleen," Mike, "Chelsea," "Brian," Mathias, Glen Hooper, "Pete," Joe Myer, Josh Recker, Matt Lee, "Mary," Wes Carter, Chris Potter, Sweetwater County Prevention Coalition, "Natalie."

1. Stolen Land, upon Beds of Coal

1. Howard Stansbury, J. W. Gunnison, Albert Carrington, and John Hudson, *Stansbury Survey Diaries*, 1849–1850. Originals in National Archives and Records Administration, Record Group 77.

2. Thomas P. Cullen, *Rock Springs: Growing Up in a Wyoming Coal Town 1915–1938* (Rock Springs WY: Sweetwater County Museum Foundation, 2005), 9–10.

3. Robert B. Rhode, *Booms and Busts on Bitter Creek: A History of Rock Springs, Wyoming* (Boulder CO: Fred Pruitt Books, 1987), 47.

2. Our Animosity

1. "To This We Dissented." Memorial of Chinese Laborers, Resident at Rock Springs, Wyoming Territory, to the Chinese Consul at New York (1885). Reprinted in Cheng-Tsu Wu, ed., *Chink!* (New York: World Publishing, 1972), 152–64.

3. With Blackened Lungs

1. Cullen, *Rock Springs*, 16, 28, 32, 37, 41, 56, 110, 147, 153.
2. Rhode, *Booms and Busts on Bitter Creek*, 126.
3. Marilyn Nesbit Wood, *The Day the Whistle Blew* (Glendo WY: High Plains Press, 2014), 189.

4. Where We're From

1. Wood, *Day the Whistle Blew*, 21.
2. Dee Garceau, *The Important Things of Life: Women, Work, and Family in Sweetwater County, Wyoming, 1880–1929* (Lincoln: University of Nebraska Press, 1997), 3.
3. Elinore Pruitt Stewart, *Letters of a Woman Homesteader* (New York: Mariner Books, 1913), 5.
4. Wood, *Day the Whistle Blew*, 21.
5. Wood, *Day the Whistle Blew*, 141.
6. Cullen, *Rock Springs*, 61.
7. Wood, *Day the Whistle Blew*, 136.
8. Wood, *Day the Whistle Blew*, 14.
9. Wood, *Day the Whistle Blew*, 49.
10. "Miners Still Digging in Stansbury Mine in Effort to Find Body," *Rocket Miner*, November 15, 1955.
11. Wood, *Day the Whistle Blew*, 208.
12. Wood, *Day the Whistle Blew*, 269.
13. Wood, *Day the Whistle Blew*, 138, 174.
14. Wood, *Day the Whistle Blew*, 16.

5. Rocket City

1. *City Confidential*, "Rock Springs: Deadly Draw in the West," narrated by Paul Winfield, aired September 25, 2000, on A&E.
2. *City Confidential*.
3. Rhode, *Booms and Busts on Bitter Creek*, 180.
4. Rhode, *Booms and Busts on Bitter Creek*, 196.
5. Rhode, *Booms and Busts on Bitter Creek*, 197.

6. At Least We Have Each Other

1. *City Confidential*.

8. Home of 56 Nationalities

1. It was, at one point in time, the biggest American flag in the country. It regularly gets torn by the wind and is taken down for repair.
2. I originally planned to conduct these interviews in person, but the COVID-19 pandemic prevented me from doing so.